TWICE
THE MAN

TWICE THE MAN

RODNEY ANGELL

Library of Congress Control Number:		2018906433
ISBN:	Hardcover	978-1-5434-8998-9
	Softcover	978-1-5434-8999-6
	eBook	978-1-5434-9000-8

Print information available on the last page.

Rev. date: 08/17/2020

To order additional copies of this book, contact:
Xlibris
800-056-3182
www.Xlibrispublishing.co.uk
Orders@Xlibrispublishing.co.uk
732217

CONTENTS

Preface ix

Chapter 1   Infancy 1

Chapter 2   Christmas When I Was A Little Lad!........................ 14

Chapter 3   Operation Pied Piper 17

Chapter 4   A Wartime Holiday 'Romance' (Of Sorts!) 54

Chapter 5   A Wartime Visitor 59

Chapter 6   A Titch With An Itch!.....................................64

Chapter 7   Strange Characters!..66

Chapter 8   The Street Fire Party, Chickens, And Eggs! (1941) ...69

Chapter 9   Taylors And D-Day, 6Th June 1944 72

Chapter 10   A Far Distant Drum Starts A-Beating......................77

Chapter 11   Called To The Sea? - Goodbye Sailor!......................84

Chapter 12   A Boy Soldier Of The King- Part 1 104

Chapter 13   A Boy Soldier Of The King- Part 2 138

Chapter 14   'All Is Not Well, Sir!' 145

Chapter 15   Brothers In Khaki.. 148

Chapter 16   A Uniformed Presence In The Holy Land! 152

Chapter 17   Good Friday In Nazareth.................................. 157

Chapter 18   The Bugler Of Mareth 160

Chapter 19   How The Fifties Started For Me........................... 174

Chapter 20   Tripoli In Another Age! 187

Chapter 21   The Night They Were Sleeping In The Mall........ 189

Chapter 22   On Leaving The Army, When The Bells Went
Down!...201

Chapter 23   Oh! For A Closer Walk With God 207

Chapter 24   Kismet...211

For Barbara, Vicky, Becky, Violet, Christopher,
John T and my Brother, John.

PREFACE

Another autobiography? Not likely! Rather, this is a collection of some memories from my childhood days which were lived through the early years of depression, then learning to accept a boyhood lived within the confines and shortages of war for six long years, and finally spending forty years in uniform.

Every small boy has dreams of what he would like to be when he grows to be a man. I was no exception, save that I had two visions of my future place in the grown-up world. Whenever anyone asked me what I wanted to be when I grew up, my reply was always the same 'I want to be a soldier wearing a black fur hat outside the King's palace or a fireman who drives a big red fire engine with a loud bell on it!'

As fate had it, I was very fortunate in achieving not one but both ambitions in my manhood, as a Grenadier Guardsman, and a firefighter (the beginnings of this career is touch upon in the last chapters of my book) hence my title of 'Twice the man'

When I retired finally from the Fire and Rescue Service, I became active in another direction for a further thirty years, by becoming involved in a variety of exciting and rewarding ventures. But that will have to be the stuff of another book, and I wonder if I would be treading on the toes of a certain Mr Harry Lime if I were to entitle that result a *'Third man'?* Time will tell.

CHAPTER 1
INFANCY

THE CITY OF LEEDS, into which I was born at 7.30 p.m. on Thursday, twenty fifth of July 1929, in the small bedroom of 1a Craven Street, was much different from the neon-lit skyscraper 'fairyland' of modern times.

The streets were all cobbled, making every cartwheel send rattles and rumbles echoing as a constant cacophony into the smoke-filled atmosphere, the result of the hundreds of mill chimneys and small coal fires in the thousands of back-to-back dwellings. If one happened to see straw laid on the cobbles outside any of those little houses, it was a sure sign that someone inside was bedridden with any of the multitude of diseases around at the time, and the straw was an attempt to deaden the sound of the cart wheels rumbling past from early morning to late at night. Not so much in the back streets perhaps, but increasingly so in the broader roads where the traffic was heavier and the houses much bigger – occupied by the more affluent families of mill departmental managers, school teachers, and the like. There was only room for Mummy and Daddy's bed in the tiny bedroom, which meant that their baby boy had a make-shift cot in one of the drawers from the bedside unit. This, above all else, forced them to search for cheap alternative accommodation.

Eventually we moved to a house in Lillian Place, Burley, Leeds, when I was about eighteen months old. The earliest memory I have of that time is of clutching at mummy's legs and asking for 'cakey-bread', a small crust of a loaf end, spread frugally with margarine and dipped in sugar! For my drinks of milky tea, I had a small cream enamel mug. (Saved broken crockery I suppose.)

I was told later that, when my brother Wilfred arrived on the scene in October 1931, my reaction on being introduced to my little baby brother was to start screaming and sobbing 'kick-him, kick-him.' There had been another little baby boy before me who died within minutes of birth, so had he lived, would he have reacted in the same way to me, I wonder?

Up to the time of getting married in 1927, my dad had been employed since leaving school in 1920 at the age of fourteen as a delivery boy, then store man, for a large pharmaceutical firm in the heart of Leeds City centre. His pay as a boy was about five shillings (25p) a week. I remember him telling me that a regular delivery he made, at least twice a week, was a large glass carboy of some liquid chemical on his delivery 'wheels' trolley. This was a small platform holding the carboy off the ground, with its body resting against the two upright staves kept apart by ladder-like rounds and terminating at the top with handles for pushing. The whole contraption was propelled along on two small iron wheels. Anything more cumbersome or demanding could only be imagined.

This delivery would take him from the centre of Leeds to the far reaches of the Harehills suburb area, a distance of about six miles. It was quite a long way for a young lad to push the great weight of a full carboy, and then push the darned trolley all the way back again, carrying an empty returned carboy from the previous delivery. Relief came from this soul-destroying job when he was about twenty one and he became a van driver's mate for the 'Standard Yeast Company', a firm of confectioners supplies purveyors in the Armley suburb of the city, this carried a bigger wage packet of about 17s 6d. (72.5p) weekly. This enabled him and my mum to get married on the twelfth of June 1927 and move into the house in Woodhouse, where I was born.

In those days there was no requirement to have a driving test in order to get the necessary licence to drive, so, after a few lessons, my dad moved from his position of mate to being a driver himself. This meant more money in his weekly wage packet and he started bringing £1 home, which enabled the move to Lillian Place, where because it was a through house, they were able to sub-let their front parlour and bedroom out to a couple of their friends, Lucy and Joe Solomon, for the princely sum of another two shillings (10p) a week, a very useful addition to the weekly household running costs. The young couple remained family friends all their lives, becoming known as Auntie Lucy and Uncle Joe Solomon, remaining as such right up till their deaths in the late seventies. Joe had a very good job as a salesman with Marshall and Snelgrove, a large city centre department store, and at the time of his retirement in the sixties he was a Buyer for the same concern.

My dad would bring his van home sometimes to our house in Lilian Place. That was my first introduction to the flag of our country, for the logo of 'The Standard Yeast Company' was the Union flag, and this was displayed in all its bright colours of red, white, and blue on the side of the van. It was a proud little boy who posed for Mummy as she took an early snapshot of myself at the age of three or thereabouts, standing with my daddy and the van. I was fascinated, I suppose, by the fact that my daddy could actually sit in a seat at the front of this big thing, and make it move along the road, giving a loud *'parp'* as he pressed the big rubber bulb of the motor horn on the side of his van door frame.

As I grew a little older, I started to spend more time with my gran Peggy (Dad's mum) who lived with the chap I called Grandad Jim, and an assortment of teenage girls (my aunties), and two young men – one was Uncle Jack (son of Gran's dead sister), and the other Uncle Edgar, my gran's younger brother. What a huge bustling family! (and only my dad was her own blood child!) I was loved and spoiled by all of them, which was a relief to my mum, who was

3

struggling to make ends meet on my dad's meagre wages, and she had another young child of three years (my brother Wilfred) to look after too. So, I almost became a permanent fixture at my gran's huge house on Burley Road in Leeds.

The basement area had a huge cooking range in one room, and another room into which, on one day each week, about five bags of coal were deposited down a chute from the outside of the house, by the coalman and his mate. They used to arrive in the back street behind the house with a loud rumbling of the coal-cart wheels on the cobbles, and the metallic scraping of the shire-horses' shoes as the two huge beasts heaved to pull the heavily laden cart and its huge pile of coal sacks. As I stood gazing in awe I was told by the coalman as he went about his dirty task, that the horses were called draught horses (or 'draft 'osses' in his broad Yorkshire tongue). One day he held me up to one of them with a piece of carrot held out on my trembling tiny hand. I needn't have been frightened because the lovely animal just looked at me with great big brown eyes, and very softly nuzzled the carrot from the little human platform with a very soft touch of hairy lips, and gave a big snort as the coalman lowered me to the ground again with a huge grin. I scampered into the house shouting . . . 'Grandma! – Grandma! The 'coley-man' let me feed his 'orse!'

I had five aunties who were living with Gran: Rhoda (the eldest), Florrie, Edith, Dolly, and Violet. They all slept in the huge attic bedroom, sharing two double beds. I generally slept in a bed with Rhoda (she was my godmother) and Florrie. Edith, Dolly, and Violet slept in the other. There were no toilet facilities up in the top of the house, but under each bed was a huge chamber pot, called a 'po'. One night there was a great 'to-do' when Auntie Florrie had an accident with one 'po' and there was wee all over the lino! Auntie Florrie covered up her embarrassment by shouting – 'It's nowt to giggle at Rodney, anyway, you shouldn't be peeping!'

All the girls worked at the 'British Screw Company' on Kirkstall Road, and one Saturday morning, they took me with them because the Lord Mayor was visiting the factory to open a new wing. One of the sheds was working, to show visitors what happened in the works, and I was frightened at first as I saw the big belts flapping and banging as they raced along just under the big glass roof. Others came down from the pulley wheels to the machines where the girls stood looking after them, while hundreds of screws of all sizes tumbled out and clattered down into metal bins underneath. I was puzzled by a little tap over the machines and caused a lot of giggles amongst the girls when I asked why the screw machines had to be washed all the time by the 'soapy water taps'. My auntie Rhoda explained that it was something to do with stopping the machines from 'over eatin'' (meaning it was getting too hot and over heating). I found that a little confusing, as I had heard one girl telling another that her machine was ready for feeding again!

Every Thursday night my aunties lined up, with potato-sacking aprons on, and Gran would allocate a weekly cleaning task to each of them. This resulted in every floor in the house being scrubbed, all the fireplace irons black leaded, boots and shoes cleaned, and ironing done for the entire household etc. Gran was meticulous, having been in service herself as a girl, and inspected every job before letting the person doing it clear up and go off to have some leisure.

There were so many in the household that meals were eaten at a long scrubbed wooden table with benches down each side (Grandad Jim had made the benches) and, except for Sundays, the table was always covered with newspaper, only being revealed in its scrubbed pristine whiteness for Sunday dinner.

Dinner on a Sunday was always a huge joint of roast beef, Yorkshire pudding (cooked round the joint of course), huge mounds of creamy mashed potatoes, butter beans, mushy peas, and lovely thick beefy gravy with the meat juices in it! We didn't have a sweet pudding on Sundays, I don't think we could have eaten any either. Before this meal, two of the girls had to take old empty Teacher's Whisky bottles to the 'beer out sales' counter at the Burley Hotel and get them filled with Tetley's bitter. Everyone had a glass, or a cup, of beer with the dinner – even me!

One summer I caught Scarlet fever and my gran kept me in bed because I became quite ill. Being the early 1930's of course, medicines were very primitive. Antibiotics and penicillin etc. were things of the future! My mum 'upset the apple cart' when she telephoned Seacroft Hospital to ask how I was, unaware that Gran had kept my illness 'under wraps' (literally). Half an hour later there was such a commotion down in the bowels of the house as Leeds City Ambulance men explained to Gran that I had to go with them to Seacroft Hospital, because I could not be nursed at home while suffering with a 'notifiable disease'! After they had departed with me to Seacroft a team arrived at the house, and after telling everyone to get out, the whole of the house was 'stoved' – a process which involved a type of smoke bomb being placed in the house with all doors and windows firmly shut – for about four hours. Gran was exploding too, only calming down when Grandad Jim suggested that the family should go along and wait in 'The Irish Duck Egg', a large back street house nearby which had been converted into a small licensed premises, complete with a tiny platform for a stage and a piano.

Meanwhile, I was arriving at hospital, where I stayed for five weeks in a bed with sliding barred sides. I can't remember much of that stay in hospital, as I was only four years of age. A few memories linger however, like the huge rocking horse in the middle of the shiny lino floor, it just stayed there to be looked at. I can't remember seeing anyone on it . . . ever! Thinking of those days makes me realise just how far medicine has progressed over the eighty years or so since then and whoever hears of a child going to the hospital with Scarlet fever these days?

Another memory I have is 'flitting' from our home one night in 1934, a common practice in those days if, for various reasons, a rapid change of dwelling was required! Flitting was always carried out at night-time, with possessions piled high on a cart, leaving an empty house for the landlord to find when next he called for the rent. However, I think we were just moving to a new house for the convenience of my mum and dad to be near the house where my mum's sister Ethel lived with her husband, my uncle Reg, a constable in Leeds City Police Force. They were fairly well off because a constable was paid £3-10s (£3-50p) a week. The house we left in Lilian Place was taken over in full, I believe, by Lucy and Joe Solomon so Dad wasn't actually 'flitting' in the usual way by leaving a trail of unpaid rent behind him!

We moved on the back of an old van, and I remember sitting with my mum and little brother Wilfred on the flat boards behind the driver's cab. (The driver was a friend of Dad's at the Standard Yeast Company.) The date stands out in my memory as it was 'Bonfire Night' and I gazed in wonder as we passed through the streets lit up with the many fires and the multi coloured displays of fireworks.

We eventually arrived at a small back-to-back house in the back streets of the suburb of Harehills, but stayed for only one night, as the house had bugs! It was a common thing in those days to go into an empty house and be struck immediately by the unmistakable smell which betrayed the presence of these horrible things. They would live in the walls, until new residents moved in, at which point the bugs immediately moved from wall to bed – jumping and crawling (for they don't have wings) – and once ensconced in the bed with the sleeping human hosts, they proceeded to suck human blood. Their proper name is '*Cimex lectularius*' but to mummy they were 'bloody bed bugs!' 'First thing tomorrow, Sidney' she said, 'we're out of here I'm not living in a house with bloody bed bugs eating my kids!' The kids being myself, aged five, Wilfred, who was just three; and our new baby sister – Patsy – about fourteen months.

We moved the very next day to Number eleven Bellbrooke Grove off Harehills Lane, a nice little back street, with about four stone steps up to the door. This is where I promptly did my 'party piece' which entailed inching my way round the railings outside the door, using the bare inch or so of the toe hold along the edge of the slab to touch the house wall, and then gingerly retreating back to safety, which I never achieved! To this day, a careful examination of the space between my top lip and my nose will reveal the minute black specks of coal left there when I inevitably fell down into the area by the outside coal chute grate, thereby driving my bottom teeth through my top lip!

Within days I was taken a few hundred yards over Harehills Lane to be enrolled in the beginners' class of the infants department of Brownhill Council School, to continue my 'education' where I had left off at my previous school (Burley Lawn Infants) in Cardigan Road near Gran's house in Burley.

What with being in the hospital and other family matters, it had been reasonably fine weather during my first experience of school life earlier that year, but it was now November! After the compulsory hour on the camp beds in the school hall after dinner (lunch), we sat on the big tufted rug in front of the big blazing fire with its huge mesh fireguard while the teacher started to read to us from 'Uncle Remus' – I cut my story reading teeth on 'Brer Rabbit', the 'Tar Baby' and company! As I sat listening to the story, idly gazing at the fireguard mesh on which the thirty or so tiny bottles of milk rested every morning – 'To dispel the chill for your little tummies!' explained teacher.

I suddenly became aware that the lights were on, and it was night outside the classroom window. Up I jumped with a shout of 'No!' and ran as fast as my little legs would carry me out of the classroom, through the schoolyard, and all the way across Harehills Lane, to my home, where my mummy listened to me screaming that the 'school people' wanted to keep me all night! It was about three thirty, on a mid-November's afternoon, and getting dark, so of course this little five-year-old child thought that he had been kidnapped! I shudder to think of a little one running across the Harehills Lane of today. There were very few cars in those days, of course, perhaps one every ten minutes or so, and then only being driven at moderate speeds!

My dad was experiencing great difficulty finding work. He had lost his job with the 'Standard Yeast Company' when we moved across the city to Harehills, and in desperation, he borrowed a little 'starter' of about £3 from Uncle Reg to get himself launched in working for himself. He scrounged the loan of a hand basket from the local butcher, and he started getting up at about 4 a.m. in the morning and walking all the way down into Leeds, where he would get all the 'giveaways' he could obtain from 'Butchers' Row' in the retail butchery row in Leeds indoor market, Dad then spent a few pence also on other items such as polony, pork pies, brawn, etc. When his basket was filled to the brim, he would cover it with the clean piece of cloth from home and trudge all the way back. After a nice cup of hot tea at home – and perhaps a pork pie! - he would set off going from door to door trying to sell his wares from the basket. This venture only lasted a short while because the folks in our neighbourhood were as poor as we were. We were still suffering the withdrawal symptoms of the Depression and although they would support him with pleasure, they wanted to obtain the foodstuffs on tick, knowing that there was little likelihood of being able to pay my dad if he called back for what they owed! Between that time, and joining the army in 1940, he had about eight jobs all connected with driving. We lived in a gardener's lodge at a big house once when he was Chauffeur/ Gardener for about three months. At the time of him joining the army he was the Lord Mayor's deputy driver. This was his only uniformed job, other than the army of course, but that came much later!

In 1935, we had one of those national events which cause a lot of happiness throughout the country, the silver jubilee of Their Majesties King George the Fifth and Queen Mary. There was quite a lot of bunting in the streets and souvenir objects in the shops, but I can't remember any street parties or any acts of collective celebration taking place. Whoever had the money to throw around on that sort of frippery?

At school however, it was a different story. We little ones were enthralled to learn why the King had changed his family name from Saxe-Coburg-Gotha to adopt the name of the castle where he lived at weekends, Windsor. We were told that during the war (1914-18) it was thought that the royal family would benefit from bearing a name that wasn't Germanic!

On the actual day of the celebration we were all told to take a spoon and a cup to school with us, with some coloured string or cotton round any handles to identify our own eating and drinking things, for the tea party we were going to have in school that afternoon.

At about 1 p.m all the school lined up in the playground and we walked in a 'crocodile' from the school and up Harehills Lane to the picture house at the top of the hill called the Hillcrest. There we saw a free film show featuring 'Tailspin Tommy'. It was a great film for the boys, and some of the girls also, I think, because Tom Tyler the air ace was in it doing a lot of stunts in his biplane. We hadn't seen any monoplanes yet, but we knew the difference while still thinking that aeroplanes needed two wings to be safe and do the stunts performed by Tailspin Tommy! At that age many of us fancied being a biplane pilot, if only to circle above Leeds, writing those big adverts for Persil and the like, in the sky using the smoke trails which issued from the tail of the biplane. One or two of the older boys used to fancy themselves at the controls sett in the gondola of those big airships that had flown over Leeds a few times; later though we were told that among those airships was a German one called the 'Hindenberg'.

When we got back to school after the picture show we found tables spread with sandwiches, cakes, and jelly and custard. If we took our cups to our teacher, we could have an orange drink or tea. It was a lovely day all round. Little did we know that the king would die the following year, and this would lead to such a lot of trouble with the abdication. That was still around the corner though, and who could envisage such things in 1935? Things were looking up slowly for my dad at work, and the tiny little baby sister born in 1933 was now a cheeky little two-year-old girlie.

Towards the end of the summer of 1935 (for reasons I never found out) we moved a few streets away from Bellbrooke Grove to Seaforth Avenue. It was there in early December that I became ill again, this time with diphtheria (killer at that time). One Saturday afternoon the doctor came to see me where I was being nursed in my mummy and daddy's bed – keeping me away from my little brother and sister. After feeling my throat, he took a glass tube from his bag and lighting what appeared to be a piece of cotton wool, he stuck it in the tube where the flame went out again, then passed it down my throat. I may seem a little dispassionate in retrospect, but in reality I was screaming the house down! I was a very frightened little boy with a very serious disease!

The doctor came back into the bedroom from outside where he had been talking very quietly with my mummy and daddy for a long time. With them standing behind him, he told me very gently that I was an incredibly poorly little boy, but I was going to a place where everyone would get me better. (I remember my daddy had his arms around my mummy. I thought that perhaps she felt faint and hadn't had any tea!) That afternoon will remain transfixed in my memory as one of the few occasions when my daddy laid on the bed and held me tightly in his arms as he whispered comfortingly to me, and read a little story to me called 'Grasshopper, Grasshopper Green' while we nervously waited for the arrival of the Leeds City Ambulance accompanied by two nurses with white masks on their faces. When I saw them, I began to scream again, while croaking and gasping as I tried to cling to my daddy! The nurses won the struggle with a desperately ill little boy, obviously! They wrapped me in a big fluffy red blanket and carried me downstairs and out into the waiting ambulance. I remember hearing Wilfred, who was four at the time, sobbing and calling out, 'Where you taking my bruvver?' On reflection I can understand my parents being very distressed – diphtheria was well known for being deadly.

I spent six long weeks in Seacroft Isolation Hospital from mid December 1935 right up to the end of January 1936, and I know that my parents nearly lost me. They weren't allowed to see me for quite some time. When they did finally come to see me, I was in a little room of my own with a blue light over the bed, because I had got a double whammy. I was so weak from diphtheria that I fell prey to a particularly aggressive attack of measles. It was a rotten time for my parents who must have been frantic with worry. I remember wondering why they were wearing those long white gowns and hoods, plus masks over their faces – it all added up to a strange game of 'Who is who?'

I had a lot of treatments administered that night. I remember one very big needle in my thigh, which bled so much afterwards that the nurse next morning had to bathe the nightshirt free from where it was stuck to my flesh. The worst memory of my stay in that place was getting a harsh smacking on my bare bottom from a nurse because, although I had asked weakly for a bed pan, that hadn't arrived in time, I soiled the bed! I can't imagine that nurse lasting long in a paediatric ward these days.

I lost out one day when I got onto the general ward. It was the custom at that time that every day the nurses would give out senna tea (water in which senna pods had been soaked) to one side of the ward ('got to keep those bowels open, you know.' Ugh!) and a lovely big spoonful of syrupy malt would be given to the other side. I had my senna tea given that day before the ward sister decided to move the beds around, and . . . yes, I got the senna again the next day!

There was a man in the ward with his chest in plaster for some reason or other, who really was very nice to me. He told me fairy stories over and over again and was such a lovely man that he gave me his Christmas pudding on Christmas Day. I had got a wind-up racing car for Christmas from my gran Peg, and he came over to my bed, and told me all about how Campbell had beaten the land speed record in the real thing at a place called Bonneville Salt Flats in America. A few weeks later, when I was told I was going home, he said he was going home also at the same time as me the following afternoon.

When the time came for leaving the ward, my new friend had to get on to the wheeled stretcher first and lie down, then they lifted little me up and laid me down between his legs. Then they threw a big blanket over us, so that I ended up being hidden from view, and trundled us along the glass corridors to the gate lodge. I was lifted off the stretcher, and the man called out something to me, but I didn't hear what he said as there was such a loud bang when the bathroom door shut behind both myself and the nurse that followed me, that it made his words simply inaudible. She took my nightshirt off and gave me a big steaming bath with lots of soapy water being poured over me whilst I stood up in the tub. Then she opened a big brown paper parcel, and I saw familiar pieces of my own clothes from home.

After I got dressed the nurse took me to a big door and knocked on it. When it opened, I was told by her to go through and across to the lady at the desk opposite. I nearly fell down as I did so, but the nurse didn't notice, for the door had slammed shut behind me! I gave my name to the lady behind the desk, and she pointed through the glass door to the gates, where my mummy and daddy stood waving at me. I heaved at the door and tottered across to them, gave a little moan (so I was told), and passed out!

To get home we had a tram ride down to the Shaftesbury Picture House, with me in Daddy's arms wrapped in a shawl. Then we walked down Harehills Lane (Daddy still carrying me!) to end up at a different blinking house yet again! My parents had succumbed to their love of wanderlust, and we now lived in Broughton Terrace at number 38.

Although it was almost the end of January, there was still a baby Christmas tree on the hall table festooned with little 'wesleybobs' (baubels) and Christmas decorations up in the sitting room. As I had been in hospital for the family Christmas, we had another little Christmas party just for me, although my brother and sister did manage to get another small present themselves, so we could be together for some festive celebrations . . . There, on the big table, was another 'Bluebird' racing car . . . the twin of the one that I had been forced to leave in hospital, and Daddy had a big grin on his face when I started chattering to him all about the race in America that my big friend in hospital had told me about, and then I passed out again!

I did not go back to school for over four weeks. Then it was Easter and holidays . . . Yay!

A couple of years later the education and medical authorities in Leeds introduced a system of Children's immunisations. We started going every month to a building in Leeds centre where we received injections. I don't know why I had to go, because if they were supposed to guard me against chicken pox, whooping cough, mumps, scarlet fever, measles, or diphtheria, they were a tad too late because I'd had the lot!

CHAPTER 2

CHRISTMAS WHEN
I WAS A LITTLE LAD!

MY EARLIEST MEMORY OF Christmas was when I was about three years of age (1932). As mentioned before, my daddy was a van driver for a yeast company in my home city of Leeds in the West Riding of Yorkshire, so he was in employment, although we were struggling still with the lingering effects of the Depression, and his weekly wage was only £1-10s, (£1-50p) just a cat's whisker away from the bread line, but we were given great help by renting out the back bedroom, supplementing the household income.

My baby brother, who was just twelve months old, slept in a big drawer on the floor at the side of my cot in a tiny little room that also had a bath in it. The WC was down some steps in the yard outside. I remember becoming aware that Christmas Eve while pretending to be asleep, of a man with a coat over his head (how strange I thought!) He said something loudly after he banged his foot against baby Wilfred's drawer, before he fumbled around with something hanging on the end of my cot. In the morning, when Mummy came to get the baby and myself, she went to the end of my cot and gave me the little orange and a shiny halfpenny that he had left . . . Wow!

'Auntie Lucy and Uncle Joe' – our lodgers, came to join us for dinner that day. Though Jewish, they recognised the importance of Christmas. We had a chicken for dinner. I was just starting to cope with feeding myself using a little spoon and 'pusher', and the taste of the strange meat was such a lovely change from my usual 'pobs' (bread and milk), which was sometimes accompanied by mincemeat or mashed potatoes. I know now, of course, that, to get us a Chicken for dinner, my daddy had trudged down on foot to Leeds City Market the previous evening (Christmas Eve), where a bird could be obtained for perhaps a couple of shillings as the poulterers in Butchers' Row sold off their remaining game, etc. at about 11.30 p.m. to midnight for a greatly reduced price before they closed down for Christmas Day and Boxing Day too.

The next most memorable Christmas (and still as painful) for me was in 1935, when, as previously mentioned, I was in the Seacroft isolation hospital with diphtheria. The dinner on Christmas day in the hospital was lovely, and I had my first taste of turkey and Christmas pudding too, I was feeling a little better by then, but I cried for Mummy when the nurses started singing near the ward's Christmas tree. But I soon felt a little better when a lovely Irish nurse came and read a story to me. Although I was not allowed to get up out of my cot, I enjoyed being in a ward with other children after the quiet of my lonely little side ward. I had a present from my parents – the previously mentioned beautiful blue tinplate wind-up model of *'Bluebird'* the racing car.

Athough Christmas for us was never a time of plenty in my early life, a polished penny and an orange wrapped in tissue paper always appeared in the stockings that hung on the post of the bed where all three of us slept. We sometimes also had one small toy each. Once we got given something called a 'chocolate shop', which comprised of a cardboard box which could be folded to look like a sweetie shop window. The chocolate shop contained chocolate cigars, and pipes, plus a packet of white sugar sticks with red ends to represent cigarettes. I remember one year; we all had a wonderful present to 'share'. It was a little tin projection cinema camera with a candle inside which provided the light to show the film slide pictures on the bedroom wall. Thinking back, now, as a former fire officer, I shudder to think of what could have happened if that candle had flared up with us in bed. The acetate film of those days also had a nasty effect of releasing phosgene, a deadly gas when ignited.

Things became even more stringent during the six long years of the war, and I can't remember getting anything in the way of gifts or toys at Christmas except one year when my mum's mum, Grandma Walton, bought wristwatches for my cousins, and gloves for my brother, sister, and me! I think we were the 'poor relations' in our family. My uncle Wilfred was medically discharged from the RAF and resumed his civilan post as the Leeds area manager for the Singer Sewing Machine shops. My uncle Reg was still a constable in the Leeds City Police, a reserved occupation which kept him safe from conscription, and he was paid a wonderful wage of £4-10s.(£4-50p) too. My dad, however, was in North Africa with the Fifth Army. His first trip out there ended when his troopship was torpedoed and he was rescued by a Norwegian destroyer. After two week's survivor's leave at home, he was whisked away from us again for another three years.

When I see the TV adverts these days for children's gifts, Christmas toys, and some tempting electronic wares too, I look at the prices and can't begin to compare the difference in cost of a modern child's Christmas stack of presents with my precious toy 'Bluebird' of the thirties. But I know which would be most valued by a little lad back in those times!

CHAPTER 3
OPERATION PIED PIPER

IT WAS 1939, AND I regarded myself, perhaps a little prematurely, as a 'teenager' during that glorious hot and sunny four weeks summer holiday from my school – Kirkstall Road Elementary, in Burley, Leeds (the school was known to all us kids as 'Kerkyroad') – for I had just had my tenth birthday on the 25th of July. My age now was in double figures, wasn't it?

Elementary schools only got four weeks holiday. But if I graduated from my present role as a probationer in the Leeds Parish church choir with Dr Melville Cooke, the 'Master of Choristers', and he agreed to me being an 'admitted chorister', I would get the chance to go to either Cockburn High or Leeds City High School (both fee paying grammar schools) with my fees paid by the Parish Church Council, and I would then get six weeks summer holiday . . . Wow!

For now I was content, and I spent many happy hours with my pals as we played 'truth, dare, kiss, or a promise' with the girls in the field at 'Old Bailey's' little farm at the end of Argie Avenue, or scampering around the streets, laughing and singing. Everyone had a favourite song, and mine went like this. . .

"Will yer come to Abyssinia will yer come?
Will yer play yer concertina and yer drum?
Mussolini will be there, shooting peanuts in the air,
Will yer come to Abysinnia – will yer come?"

It was a reminder of Italy's offensive against little Abyssinnia in recent times.

I was not to know it at the time, but those happy, carefree days of my childhood were to end for ever in the very near future.

On Friday morning, 1st September, my mum took us down to our school that was nearby, where a fleet of double-decker buses were waiting to take us to 'a place of safety' in anticipation of the expected outbreak of WWII. All the children were being taken away from the towns because of the possible risk of air attack, – this relocation of the children was called 'Operation Pied Piper' (after the pied piper of Hamelin). We all had large name labels tied to the lapels of our coats, and we carried carrier bags, little suitcases, or even brown paper parcels holding our obligatory 'change of linen'. Slung over our shoulders were those funny little cardboard boxes attached to string which held our black rubber gas-masks with the shiny round green tin noses. My five-year-old sister had a red 'Mickey Mouse' gas-mask with a rubber dangly flat rubber tube sticking out in front which made rude noises when she breathed out and caused us all to giggle. My mum kept saying, 'Rodney, you are a big boy now, and must look after your little brother and sister.'

'Yes, Mummy', I assured her with trembling lip, as I was only ten years old myself!

Our headmaster said to us all, 'Listen to me carefully, children. You must always remember that there is someone up above watching over you'. I glanced up fearfully at the top deck of our bus, expecting to meet the steely gaze of my class teacher, Miss Knapp (or 'Miss Snap' as we all called her – bless her). Of course, God would be watching us – I hoped!

We weren't very big, so all three of us were able to share one seat on the bus, my eight-year-old brother Wilfred near the window, little Patricia in the middle, and myself protecting them on the outside edge. There was a thud as the bus driver slammed the door to his cab, followed by a loud chorus of *brrrum-brrrums* and the convoy pulled away slowly from our (now homely looking) city school – with our mums, and those dads who had somehow got off work, all waving hankies, scarves, or whatever came to hand, calling out their goodbyes and last-minute reminders. We heard distant shouts of 'Be good! – We'll send you a letter and some more spending money soon – promise!' as we trundled away.

A lady teacher started a shaky version of 'Wish Me Luck as You Wave Me Good-Bye' but it seemed that not many could remember the words somehow, Miss Sutch our music teacher didn't look or sound very much like Gracie Fields either! (Did Gracie Fields cry in that song?) I was trying to comfort my little brother Wilfred and sister Patsy, who were bewildered and weeping. I tried to be brave as Mummy would have wanted, but I was finding it all a bit too much cope with also. What a horrible, heartbreaking finish to our lovely school summer holidays, but worse was waiting at our journey's end!

When we finally arrived at our destination, we all trooped off the buses in weary crocodiles, to be ushered into a large church hall. It was to be the boys' department of Kirkstall Road School during the evacuation period, but in reality, it was the Hall belonging to Otley Congregational Church. There seemed to be hundreds of ladies waiting for us. (Just like a church bazaar without the stalls!) Time and trauma has dimmed my clear memory of the precise events of the next couple of hours, but I know that our teachers' 'gavel of authority' was handed over to a band of ladies and men called 'Billeting officers', who somehow were responsible for the thinning number of my school friends and the departure of many of the other people who had been there when we arrived. Suddenly I realised that my little sister was being led away by a white-haired lady and her husband, and she was looking back at me and crying. Remembering the instructions given by my mummy, I ran after them, screaming, 'No! No! That's my little sister, Patsy, and my mummy says I have to look after her, please!' A large, bustling lady (just like Grandma), wearing a badge, grabbed me and put her arms round me while she tut-tutted.

'It's alright, pet. You and your brother will be near her, but that lady and her husband said they only have room for a little girl' she said.

It had been some hours and I was weeping by now. Gradually all the other children were being 'chosen' in numbers depending on the bedrooms 'available' in the homes of the foster parents. Eventually, only a handful of us were left in that (by now) enormous echoing church hall, with just the sounds of the low murmur of the ladies, the 'click click' of their heels on the wooden floor, and the odd sob or two from our little gang to break the silence, (it was horrible). We were given some orange juice drinks to have with what was left of Mummy's sandwiches in the neat little newspaper parcels with our names on. I knew it was hot and sunny outside, but for some reason, I couldn't stop trembling. A lady came over and asked if I was alright? She made me sit down near her table with her cardigan over my knees. My brother came and stuck his little sparrow shanks under the cardie also, and we both felt a bit better then. It was the same big lady who had reminded me of Grandma, 'I hope she can look after me and Wilred', I thought.

Time passed on, and a few people came to look at us snuggled under that big cardigan, but they also passed on, saying things like 'Only want a girl' or 'Not two together, we haven't got room' or 'Don't look very healthy do they?' Even my ten-year-old innocence finally realised that we were not really welcome little visitors. At about tea time, a lovely lady called Mrs Bagshaw (a Scot) came over. She said that she was going to take us both to her house for the night, but as her little girl would then have to sleep with her, we would be picked up the next morning (Saturday, 2nd September) by the billeting officers, and new attempts would be made to find a foster home for my little brother and myself (or somewhere else for each of us) in the area. We were not to worry as they were trying to keep us together and as near to our sister as possible.

The Bagshaw family only figured in my life for one night, but I have never forgotten the love and sympathy given to two little strange boys who were homesick, tired, and traumatised. Mrs Bagshaw tucked us both up in her daughter's comfy little bed, which looked luxurious.

Looking back over the years, I wondered what she thought when we 'undressed' for bed. All we did was take off our shoes and socks and short trousers (referred to as 'knickers' in Leeds, – a tailoring city). In those days we didn't have the luxury of pyjamas in our family, and of course, boys never wore underpants either. That is why trousers were always lined, I think! Keeping on the shirts made for us by my mummy's mum (Grandma Walton), who was a seamstress, we hopped into the lovely bed, which even had its own little eiderdown. I had never slept under one of those before – what bliss! I don't remember anymore of that night except that Wilfred and I clung together and said, 'Night-night, Mummy!' out loud, before sheer exhaustion whisked us away. Just as well really, because I needed to rest before the coming of the next day, which was to be the worst experience of all for me in the few days prior to the actual declaration of war on Sunday, the 3rd of September 1939.

'Come on, you two sleepy heads – breakfast!' Dreamily I stirred in my warm cocoon of eiderdown and the snuggled-up familiar pressure of Wilfred, and opened my eyes to be greeted by the smiling face of Mrs Bagshaw, which, although gently reassuring, only reminded me that I was in a strange place, miles and hours away from Mummy and Daddy in Leeds. As we were getting washed in the bathroom, Wilfred suddenly poked me in the arm and whispered 'Innit posh, Rodney?' as he gazed at the fluffy towels on their rails and wriggled his toes in the pile of the bathroom carpet. We had one towel on a hook in our bathroom back home and lino on the floor, but at least our house did have a toilet indoors like this one. Our friend, George Carruthers's family at home didn't have an indoor toilet and they had to go down to a yard down the street, but George didn't always go there when he needed a wee! I had seen him run out of his house to the kerb edge and just 'go' down the grid. I wonder if his dad did the same when he thought there was no one looking?

Another call from Mrs Bagshaw spurred us on. We crept downstairs, carrying our shoes in our hands, to be greeted by the delicious aroma of frying bacon and were told to sit down at the dining table, which had a lovely red-and-white checked cloth and plates, cups, and saucers which all matched each other! I'd never seen a table set out like that, except in that big shop in the Headrow in Leeds that I think was called Lewis's. Mrs Bagshaw hovered over us as we tucked in gratefully to our first hot meal since we left home the previous day, fried bacon and eggs (a whole egg each – such luxury!) followed by toast with green jam (probably greengage fruit), and hot steaming cups of tea, with nobody stopping us having more than one spoonful of sugar. During our second cup of tea, Wilfred suddenly pushed his chair back, and with a hurried 'Please may I leave the table?' he darted out of the room and up the stairs. I knew which room he was heading to, and why the urgency. A meal as rich as this was a rarity and real luxury for us and it played games with our usually calm tummies. Despite the raised eyebrows and mildly disapproving looks from Mrs Bagshaw, I dissolved into fits of boyish giggles and said, 'I think he wanted to 'go' right bad, miss'– only to receive 'I think we should be getting ready now, young man!' – from our guardian angel, in reply. I wonder if she was wearying slightly of these two little tykes with puffy eyes who had been plucked up from their homes, and whisked away to this so-called 'place of safety' and protected from possible enemy action against their home city of Leeds?

The episode at the breakfast table must have been pre-ordained for me, because it was to be the last laughter I would enjoy for some time to come. At about nine o'clock the billeting lady knocked on the door of the Bagshaw home, and after a short whispered conversation with our temporary foster mum, she took us in tow looking for foster homes again. Wilfred started to clutch my hand, so tightly that it hurt. After going from house to house, Wilfred was taken in by a man and his wife, but again we were told 'Sorry, we only have room for the youngest boy.' Wilfred did not want to let go of my hand and started crying again, but his new foster mum (Mrs Morrell) threw her arms round him and gently took him into her home, even though he tried to struggle, and was shouting after me and the billeting lady as we resumed our weary plodding from door to door in the nearby roads and cul-de-sacs.

Eventually we came to 22 Duncan Avenue and the house which was to be my wartime refuge for the foreseeable future.

After the usual long preamble from my escort, the lady standing in the open doorway said, 'Well, I suppose we could put him in our Peter's bedroom. He's away with the RAF in India, you know. But I was just going down into town for some shopping, so he will have to wait here on the porch until I get back, alright?' She nodded her head, as if agreeing with herself. I sensed that here was a lady who was used to getting her own way and did not often meet opposition!

Mrs Raistrick was a small lady, with greying hair pulled back into a bob, her stern gaze took in my dishevelled appearance and meagre possessions with one swift sweep from head to toe. My childish imagination caused me to wonder if my class teacher 'Miss Snap' might have some relations living in Otley, for here stood a lady who gave me the same sense of apprehension as she looked into my red-rimmed eyes. My intuition did not prove groundless, for she would cause me to long to be back home with Mummy on many occasions over the coming months as she ruled her home with stern sets of 'do's and don'ts'. We had come to the end of the search as far as the billeting officer was concerned, and I bet she ticked my particular box on her billeting form with a sigh of relief after she thanked my prospective foster parent for her cooperation and understanding, gave my arm a little squeeze of encouragement, and with a rather swift goodbye, – departed, leaving me glued to my safe spot outside that house!

When the billeting lady left, it was like losing 'someone close' again, and I gazed fearfully at my new foster mum with some trepidation.

'Well, young man,' she said, 'I'm Mrs Raistrick, your foster mother too, I suppose, and you are going to live here with me and my husband, and our Elsie for a while. But everybody is out just now, and I have to go to the shops for a few bits, so stay here and wait for me. There's a good lad. I won't be long.' And with a sniff, off she went, leaving me to sit down wearily on the back step of the porch amid a descending silence broken only by the sound of mooing from the cows in the field at the back of the house.

After a while, I began to feel an urgent need for the loo, but – where to go? I carefully tiptoed around to the back of the house, and sensing that the coast was clear – except for a brown-and-white cow gazing at me curiously with its head over the back garden fence – I was quick to take advantage of the drain under the kitchen window. As the flipping cow mooed at me again, getting a tired 'Aw shurrup, you bloody thing!' from me in reply, I undid the buttons on my fly. As I stood there, in grateful relief, I suddenly heard girlish giggling from above. Glancing up, I found myself being watched by a pretty pair of blue eyes belonging to a lass of my own age (I guessed) leaning out of a bedroom window next door, but only about 15 feet above my head! I darted back to the temporary refuge of my porch and hoped that she hadn't seen anything! for only one girl other than my sister had seen that part of me ever. That was Margaret Wright one day in Bailey's Field that summer, during a game of 'truth, dare, kiss, or a promise'. There was no 'inquisitive touchy-touchy' involved, and it only lasted a few seconds, but even now I could feel myself blushing at the memory! What if the giggling girl a couple of doors away had the same sort of curiosity? . . . Oh heck!

Time dragged on, and I started to wonder if I had been deserted. It seemed like a lifetime since we had left Leeds. As I sat there, I started thinking of Mummy, Daddy, and baby Reggie all those miles away back home, and started to sob uncontrollably. Although my weeping was echoing inside that dismal little porch, no one could have heard, because there was no response to my childish misery.

Eventually Mrs Raistrick returned with two heavily filled shopping bags, which she dropped thankfully on the porch floor. I don't know whether she realised I had been crying – although my red newly puffed-up eyes would have been a dead giveaway, but I stood up gratefully and wiped my nose on my jacket sleeve.

'Right, love,' she said without a trace of emotion, 'come on then. Let's see what's to do. Give me a lift with my shopping, there's a good lad. – But mind you, take your shoes off first!' Half fearful yet with some relief, I waited as she unlocked the kitchen door with much rattling then followed her into my new home.

As I stood in the little kitchen with a shopping bag in one hand, my little parcel of belongings in the other, the string of my gas mask box cutting into my neck, I was visited yet again by the uncontrollable trembling which I had experienced in the church hall the previous day. The sheer loneliness of my situation caused me to ask quaveringly, 'Please, Miss, can you tell me where my little sister is?' Mrs Raistrick turned around, and seeing the look on my face, she came over to me. She took the baggage out of my small grimy grasp, put her arms round me, and the floods of tears started yet again as I clutched at her for comfort.

'Now then lovey,' she murmured, 'your little sister is staying just across the road with Mrs Rothwell, and your brother is not far off either. So, come on now, it's time to get you seen to and settled in, how about a nice big cup of tea and a digestive biccie while we have a little chat?'

During the next half hour or so, as Mrs Raistrick sat at the kitchen table with me, I started to respond to her gentle way of finding out my name, and age, etc. I found myself pouring out the details of the last few miserable hours. She displayed a rare, gentle, motherly side of her nature to me just when I needed it most. I was to discover however that, despite her occasional sympathetic 'Oh dearie me' as I spared no details of the last couple of days, she was no 'pushover' and any wells of emotion were normally hidden beneath a very stern exterior!

The Raistrick family consisted of my new foster mum, Mary; her husband, William, (usually referred to as Will or Uncle Bill in my case), their son, Peter (who was serving with the RAF overseas) and

Elsie, their teenage daughter, who lived with them and was employed at 'the lamp works' in Guiseley. They were a small family with a very close circle of friends, and, as far as I could make out, hardly any relatives in the immediate area. This was a new way of life for me, coming as I did, from a very large family with loads of relations living in the same neighbourhood back in Leeds.

The house was very quiet that Saturday afternoon, and I became aware of the ticking of a clock somewhere in the living room on the other side of the partly opened kitchen door. The silence was broken when Mrs Raistrick (I never used any other form of address during my entire stay with the family) told me to get my few belongings together and ushered me upstairs to a small bedroom which was to be mine. I saw the little single bed. It suddenly struck me that for the first time since I was a baby, except for the couple of times when I was in hospital, I would be sleeping in a bed on my own. 'Wow! Just wait till I tell Mummy about this' – I thought.

'I'll get Elsie to help me get it ready for you later on Rodney,' she said, 'but I have to pop down into town again for some eggs, so you had better wash your hands and face and go to the toilet if you need to, because we will be away for a couple of hours, and I want you with me this time.' I breathed a silent 'Thank goodness.'

On that first day, I soon came to realise that a bus was only used when absolutely necessary, and I trudged obediently by the side of my foster mum all the way down into Otley Town. It was only about three miles I suppose, but a mini marathon to a city kid, accustomed to jumping on the nearest tram car! When we got into the old cobbled market place we noticed a crowd of people at the bottom of the street, so we went down to see what was happening. The street led down to the roadway and wide space in front of the bus station and the drill hall of the local Territorial Army unit of the Royal Artillery. This Saturday afternoon was unusual in that there was an imminent emergency, so the TA battery was exercising the twenty-five pounder field gun, with much dashing around and shouted words of command. The gunners looked very smart in their khaki uniforms, with puttees up to their knees and gleaming brass buttons.

High up on a building overlooking the bus station and drill hall, I saw two soldiers standing behind some sandbags, manning a machine gun with a longish tube, which I learned later was called a Lewis gun. I recognised what the guns were for because I had seen them in my cigarette cards collection back home. *'Are the Germans coming already?'* I wondered. After we had visited the home of a friend of Mrs Raistrick in a little back street, to pick up some eggs, we retraced our way into the market place and started the walk homeward.

'Hi, Rodney!' a voice suddenly called out to me. We turned around to see where the call was coming from and I saw the familiar grin of Jack, a friend of mine from my school. We threw our arms round each other with welcome hugs and it was a good job that there were no girls nearby to mock us as two cissies! After we had swapped our accounts of the happenings since leaving Leeds the previous day, Mrs Raistrick asked Jack where he was living. 'I'm living with a farmer at a place called Westbourne Farm,' he said.

'That's near us, Rodney,' said Mrs Raistrick with a smile. 'So now you will have a friend to play with, besides your brother and sister.'

Suddenly things were looking a little brighter, and slowly the air of utter desolation started to evaporate a little as the three of us started walking back out of town with Mrs Raistrick leading the way, and Jack and I chattering away, deep in the childish pleasure of our reunion and making plans for the next day. As we walked fairly slowly past the Beech Hill Cinema, we noticed two men fixing black tiles on the front wall of a public house called the 'Crossed Pipes'. Mrs Raistrick told us that quite a lot of men were working unusually late that Saturday afternoon to finish off jobs that might be stopped soon anyway because – 'there could be a war on, this time tomorrow!' That could account for the gangs of soldiers we had seen walking about in the town in addition to the TA gun team. My musing was interrupted by a shout of 'Hey up you two, where have they put you then?' Jack and I looked around and saw another boy called Billy from our class at Kirkstall Road School. He was standing on the corner of a little street which had the unusual name of Guycroft.

He told us that he was living with a family lower down the row of houses, but he didn't know where his brother Eddie was staying yet. He asked if we had seen him on our walk? But we couldn't answer that one. Our conversation was cut off short by Mrs Raistrick, who told us that we still had to get home to make tea for 'the family', and that included me! As we passed a large red brick building on our left Mrs Raistrick said, 'That place is Dawsons, where my husband works. It's a printing factory, but I think they are doing something for the government now – top secret stuff!' I found out later that they printed money for different countries all over the world, and ration books too later on as the inevitable wartime food shortages started to bite!

We eventually turned in to the lane leading up to our avenue and Jack said, 'This is where I'm staying. See you tomorrow then. Ta-rah for now - 'Bye, Mrs Raistrick.' He walked though some gates, and suddenly started to run up a track leading to some farm buildings.

As we finally entered the estate of pebble-dashed houses, Mrs R turned to me and said, 'Take that miserable look off your face. I've got a surprise for you.' Taking my hand, she ushered me through the gate of a pair of semi-detached dwellings and knocked on the door. Although it was only a matter of a few hours since I had been trudging around with the billeting officer, I failed to recognise the lady who stood in the doorway. That soon changed when I saw little Wilfred at her side. Mrs Morrell invited us both in for a cup of tea with her and her husband. Soon, all three of them were sipping their tea and smiling benevolently at the two little lads sitting on the settee, holding hands and chattering away happily as if we had not seen each other for years, or so it seemed to me!

All too soon we had to leave. I felt better now that I realised that Wilfred was living along Caxton Road, only a short distance from my new home in Duncan Avenue, but I still had not seen my little sister, Patsy, and I was feeling very guilty at letting Mummy down somehow. I was not to see her for another day as her foster mother, Mrs Rothwell, had told Mrs Raistrick, 'I think the little mite needs time to settle in first before she has her two brothers coming here upsetting her again.' This was my first indication of the strange rules and regulations which this old lady would impose on visits from us.

When we arrived back at the Raistrick home we were greeted by Uncle Bill and Elsie, a lovely looking, fair-haired young woman about ninteen years old with huge blue eyes, the girl who was to be my big sister for the next year, or so I supposed.

We all sat down to tea round the kitchen table, where Mrs Raistrick started to tell the other members of the family all about me . . . as I timidly pecked my way hungrily through a meal which Uncle Bill called 'welsh rabbit' but was in reality just slices of toasted bread over which melted cheese had been poured.

Uncle Bill had been a soldier in the first war, but was too old now, or so Mrs Raistrick said (with vexed looks from him), to be a soldier again and was employed on work of an 'essential nature'. Elsie was also on top secret work, she told me, and was making all sorts of electric lights and fittings at 'the lamp works' a few miles away in Guiseley (known as Crompton Parkinsons).

After tea, the two ladies of the house went upstairs to get my bedroom sorted out, and I helped Uncle Bill with the washing-up. This was followed by a little tour of his garden, which was his pride and joy, filled to capacity with all sorts of huge vegetables. I noticed that the field on the other side of the garden fence was filled with a lot of big fat cows, and he told me it was Westbourne Farm's maternity ward, where all the baby calves were born.

Later on, in the evening, after a bowl of Oxo and bread cubes for my supper, I was ushered upstairs at 9 p.m. (this was to be my regular bedtime) and found my little bed all made up and looking very welcoming. Mrs Raistrick looked slightly askance as she discovered that it was my practice to sleep in my shirt. She produced a slipover pyjama blouse for me, which I suspect came from Elsie's bedroom as it was too small for Uncle Bill and had a floral pattern on it. I was glad that Wilfred was not there to see me in my night attire, but I was missing him now once again as I snuggled down to sleep – on my own for the first time since babyhood. The last sounds I heard were a murmured 'Good night then' from Mrs Raistrick as she closed the bedroom door, and a faint shout of 'Get off me bluddy cabbages, yer sodding nuisance!' I suppose that cow had come back again to lean over the fence.

Such a lot had happened to me and my little brother and sister over the last couple of days, and I felt jiggered. We had been uprooted from our home and parents, taken miles away from all our familiar surroundings – 'to a place of safety, because of the worsening situation in Europe' and placed with foster parents in three separate houses . . . Why? War had yet to be declared, but I had got a head start!

I woke to a loud tapping on the bedroom door, followed by a gentle pulling away of the blankets covering my face, and I found Elsie smiling down at me. 'Mum says that I have to tell you to get up as it is breakfast time. Here's your clean shirt, get washed, and then don't be too long before you come downstairs because my dad says we all have to listen to the wireless soon because Mr Chamberlain is going to make a speech.' A quick intake of breath, and she vanished!

Mrs Raistrick had been through my small parcel of belongings, and taking out my one and only spare shirt, she had ironed it for me. She had then quickly washed the one I had been wearing since leaving home, and it was now fluttering on the washing line in the back garden, between a pair of Uncle Bill's long johns and a big pair of lady's knickers with elasticated knees, just like my grandma wore. Something told me that they did not belong to Elsie!

Breakfast was not like yesterday at Mrs Bagshaw's house, as I realised only too soon. There was no cloth on the kitchen table, even if it was Sunday, and the meal was pretty frugal also, consisting of porridge, sweetened on my plate with a dollop of treacle (or syrup, as Mrs Raistrick called it) followed by a fried bacon sandwich and very weak, unsweetened, tea!

After breakfast, taken with Elsie and Mrs R, I was told to go out to the garden where Uncle Bill was waiting for me with a big grin on his face. I knew I was going to like this man! He was probably in his early fifties, I think, and fairly tall with a balding head and a shaven face that always had the faint blue promise of a new crop of whiskers just beneath the skin. He seemed very tall to me, but was probably only about five foot ten and, unlike Mrs Raistrick, was very lean (not to say that she was plump, mind – just roundish!). He was a very placid man, who just wanted a nice calm existence – forever ready to pour drops of oil on ruffled waters. On the many occasions that his wife was reprimanding me for some minor happening I had only to glance in his direction, if he was around, to find the conspiratorial wink, smile, and shrug of shoulders. A willing, albeit silent ally, he kept me sane during some very unhappy times in the year ahead.

On that fateful Sunday morning of the 3rd September 1939, he stood among his cabbages in blue serge trousers, wellington boots, a striped collarless shirt, and huge broad braces off his shoulders, dangling at his side for some reason that I could not understand, other than it was a comfort thing?

'Well, son, how did you sleep then – all right?' Without waiting for a reply, he started to tell me about the cows and the field at the back of Duncan Avenue. It was a fairly big field, about the size of three football pitches, bounded on the other three sides by the Merchant Navy Wireless Officer training school grounds opposite, West Busk Lane to our right, and Bradford Road on the left, complete with the newly built Westbourne public house and loads of lovely horse chestnut trees bearing a huge mass of big green fruit promising plump conkers!

Uncle Bill informed me that all the cows in the field were due to have babies and later on in the week I was to witness a calf being born – for the first, but not the last, time in my life. Then his mood changed. 'I think we are going to have a war lad. Them Germans are not going to get out of Poland, you know. That Hitler fella is a blinking madman!' With that he suddenly laughed, lunged with his spade in the direction of the nearest poor bovine expectant mum, and accompanied by my boyish giggling, started to sing tunelessly - 'Johnny, get yer gun, there's a worm in the garden!' It was not the last time I was to hear him sing about worms either. Another one in his repertoire was, 'There's a worm at the bottom of my garden, and his name is Wiggly-Woo'

Later on, we went indoors to the instuction of – 'Don't forget to leave your boots in the porch' from somewhere in the kitchen. Uncle Bill was OK as he had a pair of floppy slippers to change into, but I had to walk about in the house in my stocking-clad feet. Later on, I was allowed to wear my school gym pumps in the house (Gran Peg had sent me a pair), but I never did get a pair of floppy slippers like the other three members of the household.

With much shushing, we all sat quietly in the living room at about ten to eleven to listen to the wireless broadcast from our prime minister. First of all, we heard Big Ben striking for eleven times, then – 'I am speaking to you from Number 10 Downing Street,' he began and then followed with a lot of information about what he had been saying to Herr Hitler and others.

Then came the reason I had been torn away from my home in Leeds, two long days before – 'A state of war now exists between Great Britain and Germany!'

'I told you, I told you' said Uncle Bill to no one in particular as he got up from his chair, took off his slippers, and after pulling on his wellies stalked off back to his garden where he started to stab vigorously with his garden fork at the compost heap, watched with concern by Elsie and Mrs R from the kitchen window. (They knew that he was remembering 'Flanders fields'.)

I followed him out to the back also, but in my case, it was to gaze fearfully at that large hill (the Chevin) which holds Otley in its shadow expecting any moment to see those big Junkers dive-bombers come screaming down to wipe out the town and all who lived in it! For the next couple of hours, I sat obediently out of the way on top of an old wooden rabbit hutch (minus rabbit for some reason) listening to Uncle Bill as he told me how his garden would be very important if 'food gets scarce' and as he laughed gently at my visions of German soldiers and bombers arriving any minute to wipe us out! 'Nay, lad' he said with a grin as he suddenly ruffled my hair, 'I don't reckon there will be much like that in Otley for a while yet.' Meanwhile Elsie and her mum were finishing off all the hanging and fitting of 'blackout' curtains at all the windows of the house, as per the instructions from the government and the local air raid warden.

Monday, the 4th of September, was to be the day when, like a London cabbie, I would start to acquire 'the knowledge' in relation to Wharfedale generally, and Otley in particular. Otley, a small market town, lies in Wharfedale, (one of our lovely Yorkshire Dales) about fifteen miles from Leeds, (was that far enough to make it a place of safety?). It nestles at the foot of a steep wooded hillside, known locally as 'the Chevin', which was surmounted (at that time) by a small cluster of stone cottages and a farmhouse/café known as 'Surprise View.' If one approaches the Chevin crest from the gently sloping approach fields to it's rear, then, the whole panorama of Otley and Wharfedale is suddenly laid out at one's feet, all the way to Almscliffe Crag in the distance, hence the appropriate name of the farmhouse/café. Also, on the rearward side of the Chevin, was the RAF aerodrome of the 609 (West Riding) Spitfire Squadron and the adjoining AVRO factory (destined to play such a vital role in the production of Chadwick's Lancaster Bomber). They were only about three miles away, at Yeadon and I remember Uncle Bill once remarked to Mrs Raistrick about the RAF station and aircraft factory being only a short distance from Otley, before adding 'I wonder who the silly blighter was who decided that Otley was a safer place than Leeds for these kids?'

Anyway, on that first Monday of the 'proper' war, I was woken by the loud mooing of a cow in the back field and the sound of crockery downstairs in the kitchen. I had no idea of the time, so I hurriedly got washed and dressed. The water was very cold, but I was to get accustomed to that small discomfort.

'Ah – there you are, I was just about to come and give you a knock. Your breakfast is almost ready' – I gave Mrs Raistrick a tentative little smile in reply (was I in bother?). She gave me a quick smile and bustled over to the small gas cooker in the corner. 'Pour your own tea out, there's a good lad, will you?' She came back to the table bearing a plate, on which sat two thick steaming slices of crispy golden fried bread done in pork dripping, complete with the lovely 'mucky bits' (which were the best part of the dripping basin, in my opinion). After adding a splash or two of brown sauce, I tucked in to my breakfast with boyish gusto! Mrs Raistrick came and sat down at the table, and after pouring a cup of tea for herself, she said 'Elsie and her dad have long gone. You will have to put up with just me at breakfast time, but that's fine because it will give us a chance to talk.' I thought to myself *'Oh heck! What have I done wrong now?'* I needn't have worried, however, because these breakfast time chats were when she 'let her hair down' a bit and chatted about all sorts of things. We both got to know each other better, but, aside from our cosy chats at breakfast time on our own, she remained the 'mistress' of the house and could be very sharp with me occasionally; – for no reason that I could appreciate! Mrs Raistrick told me that there would be no school just yet, as the premises weren't ready, and as long as I kept her informed at all times where I was going to, and she approved, I could please myself what I did during the day for the time being.

It had been decided that the girls from Kirkstall Road School were to have their schooling in the 'Mechanics Institute' and, as far as possible, the boys would go to school in the church hall of Otley Congregational Church. Some of the older boys might have to go to North Parade Elementary School next door to the church, but luckily, at ten years and two months of age, I would not be required to go to the local 'big school'. I don't think I could have coped with being separated from my brother at school, but as Patsy was in the Infants' department, I was not used to seeing her at school anyway except at lunch time so that was nothing new to me.

After breakfast, I thought I would just go to the back fence and say a 'few words' to the cows. There seemed to be more of them in the field that morning and as I sat there, on the top rail if the fence, I heard a soft 'hello'. Turning my head to the sound, I received the prettiest smile from the 'girl next door'- Marjorie.

The next hour seemed to fly by as we got to know each other, and she started to tell me about the cows in the field, although as she was quick to point out, some of them were heifers.

'What's the difference?' said this city kid.

'Well,' she said, 'a heifer is a cow that has not had any calves, and you can't get any milk from them until they do have a baby.' It transpired that my new friend was almost a year older than me and she would be going back to her own school in Otley soon, but like us, the Otley children were a little bit disorganized until things settled down and their wartime timetable commenced. She lived with her mum and dad next door to the Raistricks' and had no brothers or sisters. I liked her very much and promised to go to their house that night to play indoors.

I wasn't too keen on facing Mrs Rothwell just yet, so I decided that I would call for Wilfred and go on a sightseeing walk in the town. Jack had told me he was going down with one of the men in a truck to buy some 'stock' (whatever that was) and there was a chance we could see him. I was at that point yet to discover how large the crowds who gathered in Otley on market days were. There were people from all parts of Wharfedale and beyond, so, we didn't meet that day as I couldn't catch a glimpse of Jack.

When I got to the Morrell residence, I noticed Wilfred peeping through the curtain at the window, and I knew by the welcoming grin that he was glad to see his big brother again. Wilfred's foster parents were a lovely couple in their thirties, and I knew that Wilfred was like a little son to them by the time we returned to Leeds. Mr Morrell was a boss of sorts at the Co-op near the picture house in Beech Hill. He liked it when Wilfred and I were together, and he loved to sit talking to us. He was a very good artist and I think he used to 'hang' his pictures at exhibitions where they would sometimes be sold.

As we were going down the path to the gate, Mrs Morrell said, 'Rodney, where's your gas-mask?' She stood at the gate as I went scampering breathlessly back to number 22 to collect this vital piece of my belongings. It was a few days before I could be trusted to remember to carry it at all times, but I had a good lesson that day. As I returned down Caxton Road, I suddenly went sprawling, to collect a bad graze on my knee. Mrs Morrell was quite handy with first aid and I soon had a neatly bandaged knee, resulting in a nice big scab to play with!

We were both getting quite used to all this walking about, and it didn't seem quite so far now to reach the town. The centre of Otley that day was packed with all sorts of people, young and old. Most of the traffic was connected with the cattle and sheep etc, being transported to the Monday livestock market but there were a few khaki or green army vehicles also, and there were quite a lot of soldiers walking about among the loud chattering hordes of townsfolk and farmers too.

On the other side of the River Wharfe, from our school (to-be), lay a nicely laid out little riverside park with swimming pool, café, and rowing boats for hire. It was appropriately named Wharfe Meadows. The park gradually gave way to the sprawling acres of Farnley Park, with its endless slopes of grass and tall trees. A huge camp consisting of hundreds of army tents and temporary buildings was starting to grow in this area, and there were already thousands of soldiers 'under canvas'. This first contingent of troops was mostly composed of men from the 'Bedfordshire and Hertfordshire Regiment', all proudly sporting their cap badge bearing the stag's head (or was it some type of antelope? – I wondered).

They were joined later by Canadian soldiers who I was quite surprised to hear speaking French! It transpired that they were members of the Royal Canadian Twenty Second Regiment who were from the French part of Canada. They were nicknamed "Vandoos" and I wondered why, until I was told that it meant 'twenty- two' in French - my early introduction to a foreign language! . . .

Every day saw 'blackout restrictions' come into force, and as soon as the sun dipped in the west, those horrible black curtains would swish shut across every window in the land. Not a chink of light was to be seen. If there was you would hear a 'Put that bloody light out at number 22!' shout from the local air raid warden, followed by 'Oh, bugger off!' from Uncle Bill in the depths of his '*Yorkshire Evening News*' and finally a cry of 'Bill!' from Mrs Raistrick – with a nod in my direction. I'd heard that sort of word before, especially one

Sunday morning a few weeks' before during the summer holidays from school, after Dad and my Uncle Johnny Green had been digging all night in the back garden, putting the final finishing touches to our newly installed Anderson air raid shelter, which now was covered over by a mound of grass turfs. He dared to say to my mum (who had not had much sleep herself due to the noise and an empty space in her bed), 'This bloody tea's a bit cold Evie love'. With an exasperated snort, my mum then stood up and, picking up the tea pot, she removed the lid, and said, 'Well, this won't bloody scald you then, will it you cheeky sod? - mash your own bloody tea!' and emptied the contents over his head, and stampeding out of the kitchen, she clumped her way up the stairs, muttering all sorts of things angrily on the way to all who might be within earshot. Patsy, Wilfred, and I sat giggling as we viewed our daddy with tea trickling down his face and onto his shirt, leaving a scattering of steaming tea leaves on his head too!

Back in Otley, as Wilfred and I wandered, while holding hands, through the crowded streets that first Monday of war time, quite a few of the soldiers smiled down at us as they passed by. Some ruffled our hair and said hello, and to our surprise, we were given quite a few pennies from them too. *'I'm going to be a soldier when I grow up'* I thought to myself (how prophetic!). We found ourselves by the drill hall, but the soldiers weren't doing any gunnery today. They seemed to be packing things up in big boxes, and there seemed to be a lot of bustling about and shouting going on. Later on, when I told Uncle Bill what I had seen at the drill hall, he said 'I bet they have got orders to join the BEF.' He explained that the British Expeditionary Force was the name for all the armed forces going out to France under the command of General Gort. 'I bet nobody will call this army 'the Contemptibles' – like we got in the last war!' said Uncle Bill one day.

From the drill hall, we found ourselves being carried along with the flow of pedestrians until we arrived at the cattle market. What a din! There were cows mooing, calves bawling for their 'mawms', and the 'baaing' from dozens of woolly backed sheep grouped in lots inside iron-barred pens. The noise was made so much louder by the talking, laughter, and occasional 'hawk-and- spit' from the milling crowds of farmers. I soon came to recognise that farmers and cattle drovers generally wore battered old stained trilby hats, while most shepherd types wore a proper Yorkshire flat cap tilted to the side of their head. At that moment in time, how I wanted to wear one of those flat caps and be a country lad!

When we went in to the big cattle-holding shed with its rows of stalls, I noticed that a lot of cows had huge bulging udders, and these were sometimes oozing white milk from the teats. Many of the poor old dears had probably been loaded up for travel early that day and had missed that morning's milking sessions back home on the farm. I suddenly saw a little face grinning up at me from underneath the other side of a cow. When he saw he had attracted my attention he pointed one of the cow's teats at me and, giving it a squeeze, shot a white stream of milk all over my face! I thought that Wilfred was going to wee himself with giggling, and I couldn't be cross, really, because I was giggling too much myself. I watched with fascinated envy as the little boy produced a blue enamel billycan and filled it to over flowing from the cow's udder. Not a drop missed the circular brim.

Our new, albeit temporary friend, was a little black boy, and as I had not seen many black people before, I touched his arm for luck, (with his permission, of course . . . He didn't mind.) He told us he lived in a little village in Nidderdale and was 'adopted'. I had not heard that expression before, so he told us that he was 'specially chosen' by a missionary couple and had lived with them in Yorkshire for about eighteen months. I really enjoyed the next hour or so as our companion took us round all the stalls and explained a lot of things to us, including why all the cows and pigs had silvery metal tags in their ears, but I winced as he described how the tags were affixed. It must have been excruciating for them, because I heard the loud, piercing squeals, when the market workers manhandled pigs in to the pens, by gripping and twisting their ears - poor things!

The sheep were marked by coloured paint on their woolly coat – all sorts of lines and wiggles in blue, red, and green. Our new chum told me his name, but I had trouble repeating it, which caused him to giggle as he mimicked my 'tongue-twisted efforts. 'Heck! Just call me Freddie, like everyone else, I like that better' he said. I was very impressed by his casual knowledge of all the varied animals that day, but he was nearly thirteen years old, and had been working on a farm all summer during the school holidays. All too soon Freddie had to leave us, and we parted company with a promise to meet there 'next week'. I never saw him again, which made me sorry because I think we could have been really good friends. He probably moved away, who knows?

After our new friend left the market with his 'boss', Wilfred and I carried on for a while, wandering round the animals. I even had a brave attempt at milking, but I was very wary about the cow's bum being so near to me. There was, after all, quite a lot of cow pats in that place, and I knew where they came from!

I wrapped my fingers round one of the wrinkly dangling teats, and gave a tentative squeeze, pulling at the same time, as Freddie did, but I got no milk, just a protesting moo from the furry, chewing head, that turned in my direction. End of attempt. There was nothing else to keep us in that noisy smelly place, now that our pal had gone, so we made our way over to the big gates.

To one side of the gate's opening, I noticed an old caravan with a big square hatch in its side, from which wisps of steam were drifting to the sky.

'Get your fish and chips here!' a lady was shouting, so our boyish appetites made us walk over and peer up at the big red-faced lady who was leaning out of the opening, wiping her hands on a cloth.

'A penn'orth of chips, please,' I said, handing up one penny. This left me with five pennies (and a whole shilling!), which my grandma Peggy —daddy's mum, had given me when she said her tearful 'bye-byes' to me the previous week. Was it only three days since I left home? Gosh! As the lady handed the newspaper parcel of chips down to me, I asked her if she could spare another piece of newspaper so that I could split the portion of chips to two helpings, for me and Wilfred to share.

'Eeh, love, give us 'em here' she said, with a kindly sort of voice. After some rustling and wrapping, she handed me down two newspaper parcels of chips, but they both looked the same size as the first. I looked up to point out that she might have made a mistake, but she waved me away with a smile - and a great big wink!

As we wandered back down to the town centre, I kept looking around me so that I could become familiar with my new hometown. Street names such as Gay Lane, Bond Gate and Kirkgate were stored in my mind for future reference, and I made a mental note that there was another picture house in Kirkgate – great! Passing by the bus station, I noticed a Ledgard's bus drive to a halt at it's standing place. When passengers started boarding from 'nowhere,' I realised that they had been inside the shelter formed by the triple thickness of the sandbag wall in front of what had previously been an open-fronted 'overhang' type of bus shelter running the entire length of the bus station. The Lewis gun was still manned by a soldier behind the sandbag wall on the corner of the roof of the building overlooking Boroughgate. I remembered there had been two soldiers there on Saturday. Someone told me later on that the machine- gun post was there solely for the purpose of keeping a watch over the front of the TA drill hall across the road, and not to wait for my expected Junkers bomber zooming over the top of 'the Chevin'. Still, I felt a bit safer seeing him up there!

Being a city kid, I had a nose for finding any short cuts provided by ginnels and snickets, and sure enough there was an alley way leading from Kirkgate up the side of the squat Otley Parish church. As we walked up the ginnel, Wilfred and I took great delight in stamping our shoes on the flagstones, and listening to the echoing, ringing sound, thrown back at us from the walls.

The passageway curved to the right at the top of the slope, and we emerged eventually in to Westgate near the Beech Hill picture house. That was one to remember as we had saved ourselves a fair bit of a walk there. By the time I had seen Wilfred safely back to his home, I was just starting to get a little bit weary of the constant walking backwards and forwards; and, for the first time since my arrival in Otley, I was glad to see the gate of number 22!

I don't think we had a proper Sunday dinner the first few weeks of the war. I have a vague recollection of bolting down a couple of sardine sandwiches and a cup of tea before being sent off with a couple of apples, and the looks of Mrs R from the living room window, to collect Wilfred and proceed for our 'audience' with Mrs Rothwell and our chance to see our little sister, Patsy, again.

Patricia Ann was born on 4th August 1934. She was a very shy, pretty little girl with long auburn ringlets and a faceful of freckles – the apple of her daddy's eye, and who could argue with that? Wilfred Terrence, who was born on 8th October 1931 (which made him just over 2 years younger than myself), stood bravely at my side as we knocked at the door of the Rothwell home, and waited to see our sister again. The door was opened by a white-haired lady who invited us in and, after telling us to wipe our shoes on the doormat, took us through to her living room where we found Patsy sitting, rather subdued, in the depths of a very big armchair. Suddenly a toothy grin appeared, and she slid out of the chair to dash across the clipped rug on the floor and start hugging her two brothers delightedly – even if it was done to the accompaniment of 'Steady on, lovey. Steady on' from her foster mother, who was standing on guard over the three of us, sniffing! As our visit ticked away, I couldn't help but wonder why Mrs Rothwell kept hovering all the time, but it became clear that we were not going to be allowed unlimited freedom to see our sister as and when we would like, when she said, 'now then, you two, I think we will arrange for you to come and see your sister here a couple of times a week'. She then laid the law down even more firmly when she said 'You will have to see her here, indoors, because I'm not having her playing rough and tumble out in the street with boys. She's too little for all that!'

As Patsy started to protest as she realised she would not be coming out for her expected walk with us, Mrs Rothwell turned around and murmured, 'None of that, my love. You can see them again sometime next week.' Minutes later, Wilfred and I were stood outside the back door – end of reunion! 'Come on, let's go to see Jack at his farm', I said to my bewildered brother 'He says he will show where they keep Billy the bull.'

Later on, I would be even more bewildered than him when Mummy pronounced to the world after visiting Patsy at the Rothwell house that 'She's keeping her wrapped up in cotton wool'. *'What a strang thing to do'* I thought at the time. *'Why does she do that?'* On reflection, Mrs Rothwell was just being over-protective, and that was something not encountered before by us city kids. Although we enjoyed the warmth of a loving home and parents, we were expected to take all the knocks, scrapes, and hardships in our stride, without a whimper, because that's what life was like in 1930's Leeds. Having said that, this 'evacuation thing' was something quite alien to us but was proving to be quite educational in many ways.

Jack took us round 'his' farm and I was impressed by the amount of knowledge he had picked up in a few days. Not only did he know all the whole lay out of the farm buildings (and it wasn't a small farm by any means), he also knew the different breeds of cattle there, how to fix a milking machine suckers on a cow's udder and how all the different pieces of equipment in the dairy worked. He had quite a superior look on his face when Wilfred said, 'Poo, what a stink!'

'That's the lagoon you can smell' he said smugly. 'It's full of cow muck!'

'Oh, is that what it is?' his visitors said in unison. 'Can we go and have a look at it then!' I was expecting to see something like the lagoon with which I associated Dorothy Lamour and palm trees. But this particular lagoon was only a small field with a wall encompassing a stinking mass of brown animal manure. As we stood looking at this other dairy 'product', a man came trundling around the corner from the big shed where the cows stood to be milked, pushing a large iron wheelbarrow containing some more manure. The overflowing load, to my uneducated nostrils, seemed to be giving off a new smell.

'Ah – now that's pig muck, that is,' said Jack. The shippen (cow shed) was mucked out this morning when the herd went out to pasture after milking, I have to watch them do that job tonight – it's great!' Wilfred and I stood gazing in envy at this young farmer friend of ours, how quickly he had settled in after only two days.

'Do you think the man will let us have a go sometime, Jack?' I asked, curious of my pal's new pastime. He bent over in a fit of chortling, 'I don't think Mrs Raistrick would like that, do you?' I pondered for a split second and agreed – 'No, I don't think she would somehow, but I bet Mr Raistrick wouldn't mind me trying it, and I bet he'd like some of that cow muck too!'

Jack led the way up some old stone steps, which took us up to the granary floor above the dairy and some loose boxes and stalls. Following Jack's whispered instructions, we made our rustling way to the back of the building and some openings in the floor, and went down into a crouch, peering towards the sound of a chain rattling in the stall below. Seemingly only a few inches below our inquisitive gaze, was the muscle-rippling back of a huge cow with short straight horns, red-rimmed eyes, and a large brass ring in its nose which was attached to a chain.

'That's the farm bull down there' said Jack proudly, only to flinch back a bit himself from the opening as the bull joined in with a great bellow, which seemed to shake the floor under our feet. A sudden thought came to me, and I said, 'That bull in't black-and-white, it's a browny-red colour, and you said Billy was black and white.' Jack recovered quickly, saying, 'Ah, that's the farm bull down there. Billy is the new young bull. Come and look.' We continued, pushing our way now in to a hay barn which was open in the centre, over a covered working area with cobblestones peeping up here and there through the drifts of straw and hay. We were still on an upper floor level and were in a good position to follow Jack's superior pointing finger down to where a much smaller black and white bull stood mutely, with a chain leading from his ringed nose to a bar on the barn wall. 'That's Billy there' said Jack. 'He's what they call a yearling. Can you see his little horns peeping through that fur on his head? He's going to be the proper farm bull next year some time I think.'

'Why are the bulls kept locked up down there Jack?' I asked. 'It can't be much fun just standing there all day with a blumming big chain hanging from your snout!'

'You'll see something next week; I can tell you' he answered with a sly grin. 'Just you wait!' He would not explain further, so Wilfred and I said our thanks for such an unusual visit, and we started making our way out of the side gates of the farm to the West Busk end of Caxton Road and the home of Mr and Mrs Morrell.

After promising Wilfred that I would see him the next day, I made my farewells and trudged wearily back 'home'. The evening flashed by in a whirl of teatime, another chorus from Uncle Bill in his garden, a lot of worrying and wondering from Mrs Raistrick, until, suddenly it was suppertime. I had got quite a liking for the nightly Oxo – and I took a special interest in the bulls used in the advertising from that day on. As I snuggled down once more in my little bed, I added a PS on my whispered prayers: – 'and please look after Billy the Bull, amen.'

Later that week, I was walking aimlessly along Bradford Road on my way home from the sweet shop, not really looking where I was going, when I nearly bumped in to a cable-stitch green jersey.

'Hey up vaccy!' the owner of the green jersey said, and I found myself looking in to the freckled face of a boy of my own age, before I ducked down on to all fours and scrabbled about on the pavement to retrieve my multi coloured licquorice torpedoes as they rolled about on the ground. He was giggling as they kept evading my frantic efforts to get them back quickly before they all vanished down a nearby grating. A little black-and-white dog dashed out of the gateway of a house nearby, whisked one of my precious sweets up with a quick dab of a pink tongue, and just as swiftly, scuttled back to the rear of the house with a defiant yapping in reply to my shouts of 'Bring it back here, you bluddy thief!' This was accompanied by howls of merriment from my new acquaintance.

'You don't expect him to do that, do you?' he said, – suddenly trying to straighten his face when he sensed that he might be the next in line to get a blast of outrage from me, or even a poke on the nose. I was feeling ready for throwing caution to the wind, – I'd left the sweet shop with a precious ha'p'orth of sweets in that bag, and I was furious! After helping me to get the remnants back into the little paper bag, (snaffling a couple in the process in spite of my raised eyebrows), he introduced himself as Eddie, a local lad who lived nearby in Westbourne Grove. I was to spend many happy hours with this likeable little rogue, and he contributed quite a lot to my acceptance of my rural life in Otley.

Eddie had a rough-and-ready life at home. I met his mum, but not his dad, who was never mentioned either. I don't think there was a lot of money in that house, but I never saw anything other than a big grin on that freckled face topped off with a huge mop of ginger hair which flopped all round his head. It was many weeks later before I discovered the reason for this reluctance to adopt the more usual 'short back and sides' favoured by most boys. One day, when Eddie felt I was a 'real pal,' he let me in to his secret. He pulled the hair back and revealed the fact that he had no left ear! Naturally, he was very defensive about this accident of birth and told me that he had to put up with a lot of unkind ribbing at school.

'Not from me, Eddie – honest,' I assured him, and I never mentioned the disability again. We remained good friends throughout my stay and I felt quite honoured when he suddenly started calling me 'Roddy' instead of the scornful 'vaccy', which he used when referring to all the evacuee kids. I liked my new name, - even if I always insisted on Rodney in other places, and 'Roddy' I remained, whenever I was with my ginger-haired Otley pal.

One day I took Eddie and Wilfred with me to visit Jack at his farm, because he had told me that the farm bull was 'going to be put to a cow' (whatever that meant). He was waiting by the gate as we arrived and was almost jumping with excitement as he waved at us.

'Come on, lads, quick!, It's going to happen soon, and we have to watch from the window!' he shouted. Needing no further instructions, we all started running, and followed him through the crew yard to clatter up the barn steps and gather eventually in a little breathless gang, peering curiously at the proceedings about to start below in the yard.

One of the farm girls was stood in the middle of the yard, controlling a lovely black-and-white cow (I think Jack called her Mabel) as the cow stood patiently chewing her cud, and probably wondering why she had been brought away from all her friends in the field, although a few soft 'moos' from the nearby shippen informed her that at least one of them was not too far away. Suddenly we jumped as a loud bellow echoed round the yard, and the farm bull came into view, escorted by two cowmen, one of whom was flicking his cane in the air while the other was holding a length of chain which was clipped to the big copper ring in the bull's nose. ('Ouch' I thought with a wince.) We had seen the bull before – standing in his stall, but it was only when we saw him with his two herders that we could really begin to realise just how huge and powerful he was.

'Kutcha-kutcha,' said the man with the chain, repeatedly, as he sensed the sudden interest that his charge was taking in the cow. With just a slight pause, the bull raised his head in the air and did some peculiar quick movements with his tongue round his nose, then he started to lumber quickly towards Mabel, who was turning her head over her shoulder and rolling her eyes. I don't think she was as frightened as we all were, huddled in the window! When the bull got up to the cow, he sniffed at her bottom, then quickly reared up and got his front legs on her shoulders. My thoughts of 'Heck! I bet he's heavy' were broken into by Eddie's whisper of 'Bluddy hell Roddy – Look at that!'

I looked again and saw what was fascinating Eddie. Wilfred was just gawping open-mouthed. The bull's interest in the cow had suddenly become very obvious to us all. The man with the cane stepped forward, and grabbing hold of the bull, he helped it to smoothly mount the cow. He winked at the girl near the cow's head, and she started laughing as he said something to her, but I couldn't hear what he said because the bull gave a sudden loud bellow and got off the cow, job done.

Mabel was taken away, and a big brown cow with no horns was put in to the same place for a repeat performance by the bull.

'That brown cow is called a poll', said Jack, 'because she has no horns. The roots were burnt out when she was a baby to stop 'em growing.' This last piece of information was a 'step beyond' for me to take in at the time, because I was still trying to come to terms with my recent introduction to 'the birds and the bees' . . .wow!

After a while, we crept over to the manger drop to gaze down in admiration at the powerful beast standing below. He was rattling his chain again as he got on with his usual cud chewing. What a change to city life this was proving to be. Every day was opening up a whole new world to me. The war was a thousand miles away in more ways than one. I knew now what went on in the farmyard before all those baby calves could be born in the field at the back of my foster home. I bet Marjorie next door didn't know, and I wasn't going to be the one who told her either, no fear!

I found Marjorie waiting for me as I approached the house, and she waved me over, saying, 'I've just been to call for you. My mum and dad want you to come for your tea at our house.' That put me in a bit of an uneasy position, really, at that particular moment in time, for I was bursting for the loo! 'Thank you very much I said. I'll just put my gas mask indoors, then I'll come round.' With that I went to the porch toilet, nipped swiftly inside, and my problem was solved!

I found Marjorie's parents to be a nice, ordinary couple who seemed quite interested as I told them about my life in Leeds. At one point, I noticed that Marjorie kept giggling when I referred to my family. When we were on our own in the living room, looking at her latest copy of 'Picturegoer', she said that she thought it was funny to hear a boy saying 'Mummy and Daddy '. I thought about this for a while and concluded that, if there was the slightest chance these country folk (especially a girl!) were thinking that I was a cissy, then, from now on it was 'Mum and Dad'. I made a mental note to warn Wilfred the next day. I didn't stay long after that small humiliation, and after saying my thanks and good byes, I beat a hasty retreat back to safety!

The remainder of the evening followed its new, but now usual, routine ending with the supper of Oxo and bread cubes while we listened to the nine o'clock news broadcast from the BBC. This was always followed by all the national anthems of the Allies. As I drifted off to sleep that night, I was blissfully unaware that the war had inflicted its first terrible blow on Great Britain. The 'City of Benares', a large passenger ship, had been sunk by a U- boat off the coast of North America. The passenger manifest consisted of a lot of evacuee children, many of whom were drowned tragically. This caused yet one more reason for the world wide revulsion at the actions of the 'Nazis' and you can imagine Uncle Bill's reaction. Many more innocent cabbages were stabbed that day out in his vegetable patch!

We loved spending time chattering in the hay barn at the farm, and the next day I was back up there. On that occasion, Eddie suddenly said, with a superior look, 'All right, Jack, now I'll show you summat - how would you like to go to the slaughterhouse tomorrow and see them butchering?'

'Yes, please' said Jack, together with a duet of 'Can we come too? from Wilfred and me. It was arranged that the next day we would all meet up outside the sweet shop in Bradford Road. As we broke off to return to our various homes for tea, supper and bed, Eddie's parting shot was 'Mind on, to be early'. I was so excited for the next day I dreamed about the bull that night, and for a few nights afterwards also!

The next morning, with Mrs Raistrick's instruction to be back home by 'one-thirty at the latest' for my dinner, I set off to call for Wilfred. When we got opposite the sweet shop, both Jack and Eddie were sat on the wall sucking 'gob stoppers' and waved at us as we waited patiently for a Sammy Ledgard's blue single-decker bus to trundle past before crossing over to join our pals.

'How far is it to the slaughterhouse, Eddie?' I asked as we set off in the direction of Otley Town.

'Not too far, just off Bondgate' came the perky reply, 'but I want to call at the biscuit shop first and get us some snacks.' When we got to the top of the road by the parish church, I started to turn in to Bondgate but Eddie kept on going up the road called Station Lane. This was new territory for me and I said, 'I thought you said Bondgate, Eddie?' With a knowing grin on his face, he turned and said, 'Can you smell that – innit lovely?' It was then that I noticed a lovely smell of baking surrounding us, just like Grandma Peggy's house on Saturday afternoon's back home. I didn't need any second invitation to follow on as we went through a door and pulled up in front of a counter. The lady serving was dressed in white overalls and a white snood covering her hair. Behind her there was an open door through which I could see a lot more ladies and men working in a bake-house.

'Can I have a penn'orth of broken biscuits please, miss?' said Eddie, holding out his penny in anticipation. We were in the biscuit factory sales office and shop, and all the local kids called there more often than they visited the sweet shop. You got more value for your penny there, even if they were all broken, a penny got you a fairly big bag of delicious assorted biscuits – Yummy! The biscuit firm wasn't too bothered really about this overly generous distribution of the bits and pieces to us kids. Our pennies were only a token payment as the biscuits were surplus to requirements and would have ended up in the pig swill bins anyway. We went away in bliss, eagerly clutching our warm bargains to our chests.

'Right, lads,' Eddie said, 'follow me.' Off our little band went to the slaughterhouse off Bondgate, not really prepared for what was to prove one of the most horrible experiences of my young life!

The slaughterhouse was a collection of large garage type open-fronted brick buildings all linked together and facing on to the three sides of a large concrete yard, the third side consisted of a fairly high wall centred by huge gates. Following Eddie's lead, we all scrambled up the wall, taking hold of the many ledges and cracks, until we eventually ended up sitting on top of the wall like a row of pigeons, munching away on our biscuits with our legs dangling over the other side. That morning will be forever etched in my mind because it was to be my first encounter, to my young impressionable mind anyway, with wholesale murder!

Spread out before us was a scene of activity such as I had never imagined could exist. In the open doorway of the building nearest to us two men, both who were wearing white coats and blood splattered aprons, were manhandling a bawling, struggling sheep on to a wooden bench. When the sheep was pinned down on the bench, one of the men produced a huge pistol and pressed it to the sheep's forehead, pulling the trigger. There was a sharp *'crack'* – and except for some jerking with its legs, the woolly mound lay silent with a jet of blood spurting from a neat round hole where the gun had rested. As if that wasn't sufficient, one of the butchers produced a long knife and sliced open its throat, which created a second torrent of blood. Then we saw professional butchers get to work. In the space of about half an hour the men quickly skinned the animal (chucking the dirty fleece on top of a stinking pile of others nearby), gutted the carcase, and after squeezing the contents of the long intestines into a drain, slung them in to a huge vat of boiling water in the corner.

'Them's yer sausage skins, Roddy' whispered Eddie. I gazed at him in astonishment.

'Gerraway! Are they really?' Then I turned at the sound of a chain as the naked carcase was slung up level with the shoulders of the men, who started chopping and cutting away until they finished up with a mutton carcase such as I had seen being carted in to the 'Busy-B' butcher's shop on Kirkstall Road back home in Leeds.

We witnessd the same gory procedure with a large black-and-white bullock, but this time, the two men had to fasten a chain to the animal's head. After passing the chain through an eye in the floor and over a ceiling pulley, they heaved away until the beast was forced down with its head down near the floor. Then there was the *'crack!'*, the swift slash with the razor-sharp knife, and the whole procedure was repeated. I will always remember the poor bullock's head turned in my direction and the despairing look in its rolling eyes, which seemed to be looking straight up into mine! Eddie, who rounded off the morning by taking us to peer through the windows of the far sheds where squealing pigs were getting the same treatment, except that they were put in baths of boiling water to have their bristles shaved off before the gutting began.

After a while Wilfred and I followed Eddie rather reluctantly in to a large factory-type building near the biscuit factory as we made our way home. I nearly fell into a stinking hole in the floor, but Eddie grabbed me, thank goodness! The entire floor was covered with square pits of steaming, stinking liquids which were being prodded at by men with long poles. A man came over and started to tell us that the place was a tannery, and all the pits contained the hides of animals from the slaughterhouse. The wet soaking in chemicals was just the start of the long process before the hides became leather. Eddie looked up at the man and said, 'Is it true that you all have to take it in turns to wee in the pits?' I could have died with embarrassment as I heard this unbelievable question from my buddy. The man just grunted and walked away, I stumbled out of the doorway.

'Flipping heck, Eddie, why did you have to say that?' I asked, but with an unconcerned grin, he just looked straight at me and said, 'Well, me uncle says they do!'

By the time I got Wilfred back home, I realised that I had gone long over the deadline set by Mrs Raistrick for my dinnertime. As soon as I slid rather warily through the door, she descended!

'Where do you think you are young man, on holiday? It is twenty to three! – I said half past one – no later!' The rest of that day was really miserable. She never stopped shouting at me until Uncle Bill arrived home from work. Except for being allowed downstairs for tea and supper, I was confined to my room until I crept thankfully in to bed. My fault, lesson learned! I never forgot the last despairing look in the eyes of that poor doomed bullock either, and despite further invitations from Eddie, I never again went back to that place of slaughter.

After a couple of weeks, we started school again at the place which was to be our seat of learning for the foreseeable future. The church building was a small hall with little rooms round the edges that served as our individual class rooms. I enjoyed my time there, especially as our playtime activities took place among the dozens of cattle pens opposite on the big area across the little road. It was a brilliant sort of 'Tarzan's playground'.

The winter of 1939 was a great time for me after school. Uncle Bill had made a small wooden sledge for Wilfred and me to enjoy in the fields a short distance away, and we gleefully shot at speed down the small slopes there. Marjorie came along one Saturday afternoon, but after a couple of turns, she said 'I'll have another go tomorrow, but I'll have my trousers and welly boots on. My knickers are soaking' I couldn't help but having a good giggle at her predicament! When the snows started thawing and the Wharfe burst its banks, flooding the Otley to Ilkley Road, our little 'farm gang' descended to push cars along the flooded stretch to a rise in the road. Sixpence a car soon brought untold wealth for us, and our favourite sweetie shop owner was grateful too!

The seasons passed fairly quickly, and during the early summer months of 1940, we roamed far and wide in the nearby country side. I learned that the call of the 'Yellow Hammer' was 'A little bit of bread and no cheese!' It is a pretty little yellow bird sometimes known as a 'scribbling lark'. This became clear when Eddie very carefully revealed a nest in a nearby bush. In the bottom of the small feathery cup were about eight little eggs of a light- pinkish colour, covered with scrawls, just as if each little thing had been decorated with an indelible pencil.

'Never disturb birds' nests' said Eddie, and I have never forgotten my introduction to the 'Countryside Code'.

On other occasions we would all just lie in some field, eating our bread and margarine 'butties' rinsed down by our bottles of cold water with a tiny spoonful of sugar swirling around inside. The calls of the Cuckoo, and the twittering song of the ascending Skylarks appealed to the budding musician within me.

On my eleventh birthday, Mrs Raistrick made a little tea party for me, to which we invited Wilfred, Patsy, and Marjorie. Afterwards we were all allowed to go across the main road to sit on the lower slopes of the Chevin for two hours only, until 7 p.m after which we had to have Patsy back at Mrs Rothwell's home. Poor little girlie!

While we were just playing and rolling around in the long grass, I heard my little sister say to Marjorie in her tiny voice, 'do you like Rodney, Marjorie?' And then I went a deep red at Marjorie's soft reply, 'Yes, I do Patsy, and he is my boy friend!' Gosh . . . my very first relationship!

One day in late August, my rural existence came to an end. Back home, my mum had responded to a knock on the door to be told that as there was only her and my baby brother Reggie living in the house, she would have to provide accommodation for evacuees who needed a place of safety. I can imagine the tone of my mum's reply, for she was so unhappy without her soldier husband and three of her children, as without a second thought, she replied - 'well love, if Leeds is now a 'place of safety,' my own children are coming home to live Sorry!' Mrs Morrell and her husband were sad to lose Wilfred but happy that he was going to be reunited with his family.

Mrs Rothwell was distraught, my mum said, at losing her 'little Patsy' and was weeping as we all walked away to Bradford Road and the bus back to Leeds along with Auntie Ethel and my cousin Betty, who had come along to help with our bits of baggage (not much there though!). Uncle Bill was there to give me a big cuddle, while Mrs Raistrick dabbed her eyes a bit, of their daughter, Elsie, there was no sign. I bet she was glad to see the back of me. For the very first time in my life, I received a 'proper' on-lips kiss from my first sweetheart, Marjorie, who wept as she whispered, 'Don't ever forget me please, Roddy?' – I never have.

Back home, we were to discover that over the next five long years of war Leeds was anything but a 'place of safety'. I was happy, however, to be back in our family home, sleeping in a big bed which easily accommodated all three of the returned evacuee kids. I never got a chance to say goodbye to Eddie, he had shown me so many things I would never have learned away from the rural life I enjoyed briefly. To my regret, I never saw Marjorie again. I do hope she went on to enjoy a happy, fulfilled life, for as I promised so long ago, I have never forgotten her and our days in the Yorkshire countryside.

CHAPTER 4

A WARTIME HOLIDAY 'ROMANCE' (OF SORTS!)

WHEN I WAS A nipper, my mum and dad could only get new clothes for us by having them 'run up' by Grandma Walton, my mum's mum, who was a very talented seamstress. What she could do with an old coat, or pair of trousers was amazing. I remember with fondness my little 'camel-hair' coat for it made me feel like a proper toff and It didn't matter that it had been cobbled together from one of my uncle Wilf's cast-offs!

Mum also contributed weekly to the 'STAR' lady so that every so often she could order a clothing 'cheque' with which to purchase a new item of clothing for herself or my dad. We children only very rarely had anything like that from a shop! She kept calling after the war started and even after my dad was overseas in the army. I remember that the cheques could only be used in certain shops, and it was common in those days to see 'clothing cheques accepted here' signs in their windows. Our collector became so well known by our family that we started calling her 'Auntie' Annie. We were so familiar with her that she actually invited us all to tea at her house behind the Lyceum picture house!

One night while calling as usual for her weekly 1s 6d (7.5p), she asked mum if she would like a week in the countryside? Wow! A chance to get away from sitting in the flipping air raid shelter every night! I don't know how the holiday was paid for, but it will have been a bargain, otherwise Mum wouldn't have been able to afford it.

Anyway, we travelled by train to Keighley, and then by bus out to a place called Kildwick-Crosshills. Everything was wonderfully green, and we all tumbled out of the bus eager to enjoy our spell away from the city, which was only about forty miles away in actual fact but could have been at the other end of England as far as we were concerned.

When we got off the bus, we were faced with a long haul up a winding hill to our holiday home at Kildwick Farm. Wilfred and I kept galloping off in excitement, then stopping for a while to allow for mum to catch us up. She had our little sister Patsy with her and was also pushing a pram containing our baby brother Reggie, who was just visible behind the large suitcase perched precariously over his head on the pram hood! It was June and quite warm, so it was no wonder that Mum had beads of sweat on her forehead. In later years, when I had chats with her in her sheltered housing, she would often say that she didn't know how she ever got up that darned hill with a pushchair, large suitcase, and four kids!

When we reached the farm, we were greeted by the farmer's wife and daughter, a girl about my age (twelve). She showed us to our two bedrooms in the farmhand's cottage next door to the farmhouse. I remember how lovely and cool it was in our rooms where little blue curtains fluttered at the small open windows, which gave a wonderful view across the rolling green hills below and occasional sightings of smoke from a train on the distant railway line winding all the way up the valley and beyond! After a couple of hours, the girl, who I shall call Mary (I can't remember her name, unusual for me where girls are concerned!) beckoned to me from the farm yard below. In no time at all she and I, together with my brother Wilfred, were jumping around in the hay barn, just like Margaret Wright and I used to do in Bailey's Field before the war. Mary started to tell me about life on a farm, and the long trek she had to get to her school in the valley below, at a place called Steeton.

'It must be great to live here with all these sheep and cows and chickens' I said. I knew about chickens, of course, as I had my own poultry run at home. However, I had never seen the grey-and-white speckled birds with little red-wattle-shrouded heads before. Mary told me they were called 'Guinea Fowls'- 'lovely juicy meat on 'em' she said, with a grin. They just ambled around in the barn area all the time, seemingly aloof to the other poultry.

'Aye, it's grand 'ere in't summer, but bluddy 'ard in't winter!' she replied to my question. I'd never heard a girl swear before, but I accepted that it must be the way they spoke out there in the countryside.

After a while, she told us to sit down in the hay as she was going to tell us 'summat speshal' With a mysterious look on her face, she told us that a film company had been to the big house along the hill top ('Kildwick Grange') some time before the war started, to make a film called 'Wuthering Heights' and they had included a part where a ghostly hand raps on a bedroom window to get in. When Mary saw that she had our full attention, (Wilfred and I were huddling together for mutual comfort at the mention of ghosts) she started to embroider the story by telling us that the film-makers had used the windows of our cottage bedroom for the ghostly hand scene, because there were no windows in the big house of a suitable small size. It was all nonsense of course, as I realised later, but she had put Wilfred and myself in fearful dread, as we prepared for bed that night. At the first sound of the wind on our window, we both huddled together under the bed clothes until sleep took over and whisked us both away to the safety of dreamland.

The next day, Mum had arranged a special trip for us to a cinema in Keighley. Off we went trundling down that hill, less suitcase this time, thankfully for Mum. At the bus stop, we saw a man in a black battle-dress blouse with a big yellow diamond patch sewn on his back sitting on the wall of a nearby field. He smiled at us kids, and then helped Mum to get the pram on to the bus before hopping over the small wall to join a few more men, all dressed like him, working in the hay field. That friendly man gave us our first encounter with a German POW, and I began to realise that not all Germans were monsters! I remember to this day that visit to the cinema in Keighley, because of the way the name was spelt - 'Kozy Kinema.' The film was a musical, the Gilbert and Sullivan opera 'The Mikado', which Mum loved. I had only seen one long Technicolour film before, and that was back in 1937, when Grandma Walton had taken us all to the Lyceum Picture House to see 'Snow White and the Seven Dwarfs', Walt Disney's first full-length animated film in technicolour.

That night we told Mum that a ghost might come knocking again on our window, so after telling us how daft that story was, she let us get into her big double bed with her. Little Patsy and our now three year old brother Reggie were at the other side of her room in a single bed. It was warm and so cosy in Mum's bed, and we felt so safe with her as we fell asleep, until – 'Rat- a - tat-tat- rat- a- tat -tat' came the sound at the window. It was just loud enough to send both Wilfred and me scrambling under the blankets with cries of 'It's the ghost! – It's the ghost Mummy!' After telling us to shush while she investigated the sound and its cause she opened the window, and leaned out, saying, 'Hello! Is there anyone there?'.

'Thank goodness' came a man's voice from below. 'It's Syd, I've been chucking damned pebbles up at the window for ages!'

'It's your dad, he's come home on leave,' said Mum, turning away from the window to go downstairs, where she let the tired soldier into the room downstairs. He gave us all a big cuddle as he said to Mum, 'I've had to walk all the way from Keighley, no joke, with a kitbag on me shoulder!' We had to vacate Mum's bed, of course, but we didn't mind braving any further ghostly tappings now that our daddy was home to see 'em off!

The rest of the holiday was wonderful, as we were a little family again, if only for a few days. We went for long walks across the moors most days, one day we even tramped as far as the tall stone cairn and cross which stands on the skyline above the village of Settle down in the valley below.

We all enjoyed playful romps in the hay barn along with our new friend Mary also. She wore pink bloomers down to her knees, as I notice during one mad wrestling match. I wondered if that was a country way of dressing, as all the girls I knew back home wore the smaller gym style dark-blue shorter-legged knickers. We learnt all sorts about the countryside and it's residents during that week away, which will remain pleasant childhood memories.

All good things come to an end of course. On the Saturday we had to set off for the final time down that hill again. Dad was pushing the pram this time for a relieved Mum; I was quite tearful really, for we were going back to our nights in the air raid shelter, Dad was going back to the army in a couple of days, and I was going to miss our wonderful games in the hay barn with Mary. She had given me a quick 'good bye' kiss on the lips, just as Marjorie did when I left Otley, so was that my first encounter with what is called a 'holiday romance'? Probably not, when it only involved two twelve year old kids, but I bet Mary remembered that week for a long time afterwards, as I did. I drove past that spot overlooking Kildwick once in later years, and I looked at that old farm-house and its hay barn with a fond smile as I remembered that week of long ago, and the holiday with Mum, Dad, my brothers, little sister, and of course - dear Mary!

CHAPTER 5

A WARTIME VISITOR

WHEN I CAST MY mind back over the eighty years or so that have 'flown' by since we were at war on the 'Home front' (as Churchill called it), the oddest memories come back, and I sometimes sigh, giggle, or even blush! (tell you why sometime) as I recall incidents that may have been lying dormant in some corner of my mind, just waiting for an opportunity such as this to come to life again. Where to begin? – Oh, I know! . . .

There was great excitement one day in the early spring of 1941 at Kirkstall Road Elementary School, which is the school I attended in those days. I believe it is known as Kirkstall Valley School now. The Lord Mayor of Leeds was coming to the school on an official mayoral visit. He was going round all the schools in Leeds to talk about the war, and what we, as children, could do to help our mums cope with the increasing worries and burdens of running a house and family, while our dads were away fighting overseas.

On the morning of the visit we had a rehearsal in the assembly hall for that afternoon's proceedings. The girls department came up to join us from the floor below. I don't think my little sister Patsy had got used to the segregated system practiced at the school, although when we were in Otley as evacuees, the girls and boys had been going to different locations for their schooling! There was a platform against one side of the hall with some chairs on it, and we all gazed at it with looks ranging from awe to indifference, as we were pushed and pulled by harassed staff, who became more short tempered when things didn't just fall into place. I ducked as there was a swish of an arm near my head followed by a sharp *'slap'* as the boy next to me got a crack across the head for not responding quickly enough to the impatient orders of one short- tempered lady teacher. There was a wave of childish giggles when the rather portly figure of Miss Sutch mounted the platform with a piece of white paper on her chest which proclaimed her to be 'the Lady Mayoress.' I spent a few moments wondering, before I realised that the paper notice was held in place by safety pins. (Cellotape was to be an invention a long way in the future!) After Miss Sutch had been sitting there for a few moments, the head master, Mr Winfield, realised that 'the Lady Mayoress was also 'the lady pianist' so the label of Lady Mayoress was switched to the chest of Miss Knap or Miss 'Snap'!

There was much giggling among the girls (and some boys too) not used to singing en masse like this. I was a choirboy and a bit of a goody-goody when it came to singing though, and I really enjoyed the increased sound of about two hundred and fifty voices, as we sang the two songs – 'All Through the Night' and 'Oh No, John!' I was a little bit disappointed though when some teacher had the bright idea of getting the girls to sing the lines 'Oh no, John; no, John; no-o, John -no!' because I always liked to give those lines some 'gusto' myself. But I think it pleased the headmaster, Mr Winfield, because his head was nodding in time to our singing -I didn't know his head moved!

At dinnertime (Yorkshire folk didn't know then what the term *'lunch'* meant) I went with my brother Wilfred into the classroom of Mr Smith, the class teacher for junior 4. We had a few men teachers who were either too old to be in the forces, (Mr Martin of senior 4 had been in the first war) or were unfit to serve.

Mr Smith was a nice man, and was always kind to us, especially little Patsy, who used to come up to join us at dinnertime, as I had our sandwiches in a newspaper parcel in my desk. I remember once he gave Patsy a drink from his bottle of Tizer, which made a nice change for her from the big bottle of 'sugar water' which we brought to school with us. He made her giggle when he teased her about her freckles, asking her if someone had dropped her in a bran-tub at the Sunday school bazaar?

Unlike Wilfred and I, who had very dark-brown hair and fresh faces (which scrubbed up quite pink!), Patsy had a mass of beautiful auburn ringlets, which mum used to tie up in bits of rag every night at bed time, and hundreds of freckles all over her face. Our little baby-brother Reggie was of a similar colouring to Patsy, which caused my grandma Walton (Mum's mum) to declare 'little Patsy and baby Reggie are proper Waltons they are!' and, of course, this would draw a riposte from my grandma 'Peggy' in a broad Shropshire accent: 'Aye! an' they two bonny lads they be true Angells, they be!'

They didn't see eye to eye, and my gran Peggy, would often refer to my gran Walton as 'Old Mother Walton'! at which gran Walton would just sniff, and hum a snatch of a hymn from 'Sankey's book of sacred Songs and solos' ('Er woz a fervent Congregationalist her woz!' . . . Bless her!) as she got on with her sewing. She was a seamstress and worked at home, making suits for ladies and gentlemen.

In the afternoon at about half past one, we all marched into the assembly hall. The girls' school first, followed by the rest of us, in strict order of classes from junior 1 up to senior 4, while Miss Sutch bashed out the march 'Blaze Away' on the piano. (In a few years' time I would think of her now and then when we played that particular march in the Guards.) There was a lot of shuffling around until both schools were sitting cross-legged on the floor in various formations, but all facing the 'mayoral' platform. The girls were very conscious that try as they might, there was no way they could hide their knickers from the giggling boys, although they had no qualms about hoisting their skirts up to get their hankies out of the knickers pockets! I don't know why girls made such a fuss about things like that. Most boys had no interest at all in girls at that age, and I, for one, never thought about girls' knickers anyway!

At about two o'clock, there was a whispered command of 'All stand!' from the back of the hall, and hundreds of children pushed and shoved themselves into a standing posture of sorts, while Mr Winfield led a small procession of people on to the platform. When they were sitting down, the same voice from the back hissed 'All sit!' There we were, back in our original positions, with our eyes now transfixed on an old man in a long Santa Claus coat, wearing a lovely big golden chain round his neck, and a lace hankey like a baby's bib at his throat!

Mr Winfield said a few words of welcome, and told us who the Lord Mayor was and what he did, and he said he was sure that the important visitor would just love to hear us sing 'Oh No, John' – *'bet he doesn't know it'* I thought to myself, only to be proved wrong when he started joining in with the girls when they sang their bit 'Oh no, John' with Mr Winfield nodding along at his side!

Then the great man got up to speak – 'Good afternoon, boys and girls'- and like a bomb-burst, with no warning, there was the loudest noise I had ever heard in my life and the world exploded! Or so it seemed. There was a tremendous explosion which shook the building, shivered the floor on which we were sitting, and rattled the windows, which, fortunately, were all covered with gauze to stop them shattering at such a time as this. I hadn't heard the air raid siren, or any aircraft noise either, and we could all certainly recognise the *'thrum-thrum-thrum'* of their engines after spending every night in our cellars or air-raid shelters at home. By that stage of the war, we boys were all beginning to boast of our so–called skill of recognising the noise of the planes which were passing overhead heavily laden with bombs, to the noise of those lighter enemy planes on their way home. The engine noises were noticeably different in tone. Unlike boys before the war who swapped cigarette cards, we were avid collectors of shrapnel. I remember being the envy of every boy in the playground, when I proudly showed off the nose cone of an anti-aircraft shell which I had found in our back garden, it had missed my little chicken shed, thank goodness.

When the noise subsided, except for the sobs of lots of frightened children (me amongst them!) the headmaster, for some reason known only to himself, decided that the entire school should be taken downstairs and out on to the main playground fronting Kirkstall Road. Perhaps he thought the school building was in danger of collapse – who knows?

However, when we were all out on the front playground, worse was to come for us, as if we weren't already traumatised enough. Kirkstall Road at that time was about forty-five feet across. On one side was our sloping tarmac playground, still with its railings at that time, and on the other side of the road was a range of single-storey factory buildings which extended for about five hundred yards towards Leeds. Facing us about one hundred yards away was a big broken-down shape of a building with blackened walls, from which were pouring plumes of smoke and flames skywards.

A lady teacher suddenly screamed, and pointed upwards to where, in front of the unbelieving eyes of hundreds of horrified children, a smoking body was hanging face downwards over the tram wires! What happened next has blurred with the passage of time but I do remember my mum running across the playground of the school grabbing Pasty, Wilfred and me in her arms, while she saying, 'Thank God, Thank God!'. Along with lots of other frantic parents, she assumed a bomb had dropped on the school.

The Lord Mayor called for an immediate investigation and it transpired that a shell-filling factory had been allowed, by probably the Ministry of Munitions, to be opened in a zone that was normally severely prohibited because of its proximity to a school.

It transpired that there had been an explosion, which caused massive damage to the factory. Sadly, but fortunately, this resulted in only a light loss of life which included the sad victim across the tram wires. We were told later that she was an auntie of one of the horrified children standing in the playground of Kirkstall Road school.

That day, we were not only visited by the Lord Mayor, but the war came calling too!

CHAPTER 6

A TITCH WITH AN ITCH!

DURING THE DARK DAYS of WWII, Leeds was struck with an epidemic of scabies. This is a nasty skin complaint caused by an evil little crablike thing which burrows away under one's skin, causing severe itching and cracked skin. It wasn't caused by dirt, as some folks thought, but by the deficiencies in our restricted wartime diet. It was terribly contagious and could be passed on by something as simple as shaking hands or the exchange of money. It was a miserable infection which caused embarrassment to all young and old.

At that time, scattered throughout the city, buildings were converted to 'gas cleansing stations'. These consisted of several rooms with baths and changing areas. After receiving a call from the health department, an entire family would go to such a station at night. They would carry a change of clothing for wearing after the treatment. The clothing worn on arrival was left for fumigating and collected at a later date.

The ladies and men were shown to their changing rooms. After stripping off and leaving their worn clothes on the floor, they were taken into a room with about three baths full of steaming hot water. This must have been terribly embarrassing for all concerned.

When it was our turn, I remember being taken into a bathroom with my brother and another boy, and after being scrubbed clean in a bath of very hot soapy water (and I do mean scrubbed!) we were towelled off by a nurse wearing gloves. Then we had to stand in a line while she 'painted' us all over using what I can only describe as a decorator's emulsion brush, which she kept dipping in to a huge pail containing a thick white viscous liquid of sorts which she applied liberally all over our bodies. This included the bare soles of our feet, which we lifted at her command like tame horses at the farriers!

Now at that time, I was almost fifteen years of age, and becoming aware of certain changes in my boyish physique. I drew myself up to full height of about 'five feet and a gnats spit', drawing in my tummy tightly, and sticking out my skinny chest trying to look as grown up as possible. Feeling manly, and a little too confident, I looked her full in the face and gave her what I thought was a friendly wink. She didn't seem particularly impressed however and finished the job in hand without batting an eyelid.

Is there a moral to this tale? Well, I suppose you could say 'Don't flaunt your eggs until they're ready for hatching'.

CHAPTER 7

STRANGE CHARACTERS!

I HAVE ENCOUNTERED MANY characters in my life but there are four that stand out and therefore surely deserve a mention in my memoirs.

When I was a youngster, in the days before immigration, there was only *one* coloured man living in my area of Leeds that I can remember. He played a banjo on street corners with a battered top hat at his feet to collect the odd coppers that folks, who probably had less money than him, would drop in in return for him playing a song which they had requested. I thought all his tunes sounded the same and although he may have had differing words for each rendition, it was hard to tell them apart, but his lovely smile never wavered. As children we believed that if we could touch his coat, we would be sure to have good luck . . . someday!

Someone else that I remember was an 'oldish' lady who stood at the same corner of a building on Wellington Street in Leeds - for most of her life, it seemed. She was there when I was peeping through the tram window as I made my way to my grammar School on the other side of Leeds in the forties (there were a few peep holes through the shatterproof gauze during the war) and she was still stood there until the late fifties. She wore old army boots tied with string at the bottom of her bare, dirt-streaked bandy legs, with an old ragged khaki greatcoat for some warmth, and a railway porter's cap. She would accost passers-by for fags, earning herself the nickname of 'Woodbine Lizzie'. Woodbines being amongst the cheapest brand of cigarette. When unable to 'cadge' (a Yorkshire term for obtain) a smoke from passers-by she wasn't averse to picking up any discarded fag ends out of the gutter for the occasional puff!

The male equivalent of Woodbine Lizzie was a chap I came across during my time as an evacuee in Otley at the beginning of WWII. He was one of Wharfedale's 'gentlemen of the road'. He always wore a bowler hat and an old army greatcoat, which he had probably scrounged somehow from the sprawling army camp that occupied the slopes of the hillside. His boots had straw peeping from the tops instead of socks, and he exuded a definite whiff of camphor wherever he wandered because his coat pockets were always bulging with mothballs - for some strange reason which no one could explain. This of course resulted in his given nickname - 'Mothballs'! The 'vaccys' (as the local children called us evacuees) would follow the strange old man for a short distance occasionally, because for a greeting of 'Hello, Mr Mothballs!', he would give a benevolent smile revealing brown stumps of teeth, and give each of us one of those smelly white balls of camphor. Local rumour had it that he was the 'black sheep' of a titled family who had been disowned and cast out to take to the road, but I doubt that. The one other thing that I remember about him apart from his strange ways and dress, was the *'Flap! Flap!'* sound he made as he shuffled along his way. This was caused by one of his boot soles 'laughing' as we called a sole that was hanging adrift!

The final 'character' who earnt his place in my memories was the tiny dwarf-like shoe shine boy I encountered during my days as a young grenadier serving in Libya during the late forties. He had a box fitted so he could be encased with the 'workshop' of his calling. He propelled himself along with his hands only, for he had no legs. His tiny upper torso supported a large head surmounted with a red 'tarboosh' and fluffy black tassel, the Libyan version of a fez. When sitting outside one of the many bars, (for drink was still allowed in Tripoli at that point, these were the days the Senussi Arabs threw off the yoke of their Italian former lords and masters' and Gadhaffi came to power) he would shuffle up and ask for our custom. If one of us agreed to have a shoe shine, he would get his customer to place each foot in turn on top of his body box, and after opening a drawer he would impart a mirror-like gloss in exchange for a few lira, although he was not averse to a few cigarettes instead. I heard that there was chaos caused one day at another bar, when a matelot on shore leave picked up the poor little shoe shine boy and plonked him, box and all, on one of the bar stools before sauntering away, with the enraged screams of Arabic curses following him through the reed curtains!

CHAPTER 8

THE STREET FIRE PARTY, CHICKENS, AND EGGS! (1941)

DURING THE WAR, THE NFS (National fire sevice) in Leeds created 'out stations' to provide fire cover for the city. In many cases these posts were manned by about ten crew members with only an old truck pulling a trailer pump, so it was decided to create civilian firefighting teams to aid their efforts. These teams were mostly women, and each street had a few folks equipped with blue steel helmets bearing the white letters FP (fire party), a stirrup pump, a metal scoop on a long pole and two buckets of sand. A fireman visited each neighbourhood and gave training on how to tackle incendiary bombs.

I was so proud when I heard that, during one air raid practice session, my mum had tackled an incendiary bomb in the street by crawling along with another lady and, using the scoop, managed to circle the magnesium incendiary with sand and watched until the imaginary flames died out! It was only a dummy bomb, but I am sure she would have been able to cope with a real one! We had one drop in the street near our back gate during one raid, but it was a dud, I think. The fire brigade sent a truck out to pick the menace up and dealt with it. I saw it when I went out in the early morning to see if there was any shrapnel for me to collect for swapping at school! One morning I found the already mentioned nose cap from an AA shell in our back yard, a great find!

Because there was such a sense of 'togetherness' during the war on what was called 'the home front', the fire folks in our street formed a little social club which met in a different house once a month for a little social evening. It would take more than a war to get us down, for we civvies were of 'the British bulldog breed'!

At the time, although I was only twelve years of age, I had a chicken run on the edge of a nearby village which housed a couple of dozen pullets and a cockerel. I made all the nesting boxes, dropping boards and perches myself from wood I scrounged from shops and a joiner's yard round the corner. I used to take the family ration books down into the city, where I would produce them for the Food Office staff and have every page stamped PK (Poultry Keeper) over the egg coupons in the books. This meant we had decided to give up our egg rations in favour of obtaining chicken feed instead at the grain store or in my case, the local co-operative store. I would go once every two weeks and buy a stone (14 lbs.) of balancer meal, which I would mix with boiled potato peelings each evening for the chickens' scoff time!

Alongside their food, I would often put a spoonful of cod liver oil in their food trough and I would add ground up sea shells and any broken crockery. This was needed by the birds to store in their crops (the chicken crop is located beneath the neck and is the first part of a chicken's digestive tract) for grinding up their food, and also for providing the necessary calcium for egg shell production! I developed a bit of knowledge too about chicken husbandry. When I had an attack of red mite in the chicken house, I learned to treat and cure the problem by 'painting' each bird's legs with paraffin borrowed from the heating stoves in our basement air raid shelter. I also had to write to the Ministry of Food and Fisheries in St Anne's in Lancashire to obtain the necessary docket to buy a roll of wire netting (we were at war of course) when the chicken run fence needed repairs. What an education I had through the vagaries of war!

One day, when it was my mum's turn to host the fire party social evening in our living room, she asked me if I could spare an egg for the raffle prize? After a bit of hesitation from this 'poultry farmer' (and a clip round my ear from Mum!), I donated one lovely brown egg, if reluctantly, from one of my Rhode Island red pullets. It seems unbelievable now that a thing as humble as one lone brown egg could be the precious sole prize of a raffle, but when compared to the monthly ration of one small egg per person, it wasn't a bad prize at all. The money raised by the raffle, usually about 1 *shilling* (5p), went in to the tea fund. The 'tickets' were bits of paper cut up by my mum, with handwritten numbers on them, and were a ha'penny each (1p). Sometimes she would play the piano for a little sing-song and she generally got me to sing something for the group aswell, this would usually be 'Hear My Prayer' or 'The Old Rustic Bridge by the Mill' and as I was still a boy soprano then my solos would come complete with trembling knees!

My uncle Reg, a Leeds City Police constable, and my uncle Wilf, who had been discharged from the RAF after being run over by a runaway aircraft wheel, both kept chickens too, but it was this blood thirsty thirteen year old who dealt with the family poultry preparations for Christmas. I developed a knack for killing, plucking, and drawing the birds; and I could have a dozen birds hanging in our cellar ready for the table. My uncles paid me 6*d* (2.5p) per bird for my services – very nice, thank you. I got just a clip around the ear as usual when I tried to charge my mum the same for preparing our own birds!

Life on the 'home front' during WWII had it's lighter moments, just a few!

CHAPTER 9

TAYLORS AND D-DAY, 6TH JUNE 1944

WHEN I STARTED MY Easter break from grammar school in 1944 I had no intention of leaving school forever, but that is precisely what happened.

The reason escapes me now but when the members of my form returned to that place of learning on the Wednesday after the Easter weekend (we had the minimum of holiday breaks in those days) my seat was empty. This was because I was already at work in the 'dry drugs' department of Taylors Drug Company in Leeds having been encouraged by the bland assurance of the personnel manager, that if I applied myself to the company routines and my studies, I would eventually be able to have my own chemist's shop and the suffix MPS (Member of the British Pharmaceutical Society) to my name!

The room I worked in was vast and covered a huge floor area and was devoted to the making up of orders placed by the company's branches, which were then sent, via the despatch department loading bays, for delivery. One half of the floor (which I worked in) specialised in collecting and wrapping the dry drug components for the orders, and the other half of the floor the 'wet' drug components. The factory had many other smaller buildings connected with the manufacture of a multitude of drugs. These were dotted about in the fairly large area of land occupied by the factory at the top of Burley hill, not far from my home.

I worked from 8 am to 5 pm weekdays and 8 am to 12.30 pm on Saturdays for which I was paid 12s/6d per week (52.5p). Each Friday evening, I would give my little brown wage packet to my mum and she would in return give me 2s/6d. (22.5p) back for my pocket money. Giving her this little pay packet was with a certain amount of reluctance on my part because I knew that she was getting a princely wage for her war work at Thackwray's making surgical tubular steel furniture for the military hospitals. When I quizzed her about handing over my hard worked for funds, she explained that my small amount of money going in the 'pot' was a token of me contributing to the family needs. It took a while for me to accept that reasoning, but I supposed Mum knew best!

Thinking back, there must have been a fair amount of money coming into the house though because we always had two soldiers lodging with us from the government training centre (GTC) in Kirkstall Road where they were taught to be fitters, and turners, etc. The Soldiers were from a new corp of the army and their cap badges consisted of a brass circlet surmounted by a crown, and at intervals around the circlet were the initials R.E.M.E. (Royal Electrical and Mechanical Engineers) They also had a newly established rank, for they weren't called Privates, but 'Craftsmen' - later to be known light-heartedly throughout the forces as 'crafties'. Although an infant corps then, the R.E.M.E was to establish itself a valuable niche in the army, which I came into contact with many times myself during the course of my military life – a few years hence.

When we weren't housing soldiers, we would house two ATS girls from the Royal Army Pay Corps, who worked as clerks at the large army pay office in Leeds. I liked having the ATS girls because they were always friendly, and to me they held a certain youthful attraction. In my memory I thought they were all very pretty even if they weren't, and their easy-going manner upstairs when they were getting ready to go on duty, meant that I often saw them wandering around in a state of undress. They weren't issued with very glamorous underwear, and their thick khaki stockings, coupled with long khaki bloomers with elastic below the knees, were a sure way of deterring any incipient youthful voyeurism in my early years of growing up. Like many other boys of my age, I had the occasional day dream, and they were sometimes accompanied by visions of those young lassies in their horrible, yet feminine bloomers – oh flipping heck!

My working hours at Taylors' were long and hard, and I was the junior member of the team of three. My two work companions were Mary, a lovely motherly lady who had worked at Taylor's since she left school, (she had finished for a few years to have a baby before returning when the little lass started at school) and a man called 'Jimpy' by most people. He would normally have retired 'but for the war'. He didn't say a lot, but he was determined that I would learn the job and he had a very gentle way of telling me many of the bits of information that he had acquired over the years since he left school, and started work in that very department just like me. After a few days I found out that his real name was Richard and that 'Jimpy' was a rather cruel nickname he had borne since his schooldays because of the large medical boot he wore to correct the shortness of his left leg which caused him to walk with a pronounced limp. Mary and I called him Richard, as did our supervisor, but to everyone else 'Jimpy' he had always been and would remain so! He didn't seem to mind, perhaps he thought that since he had carried the epithet from school, what was the point of trying to change things now.

All three of us were under the supervision of a man called Mr Simpson. Aside from checking all our made-up orders, before I took them to despatch in the trolley, he spent most of the day behind the locked door of his little glass walled 'Dangerous Drugs' office in the corner doing his own very vital work, identified by the warning notice on his door. I never took anything from him to despatch as he would take all his bottles and boxes of orders himself, in a locked steel box down to a 'specified' department somewhere downstairs in the offices area.

Part of my job was to pick up the outlying branch chemists' dry drugs demand dockets from the general office each morning, and then take them to Mr Simpson, who would look through them all, sometimes scoring something out with a red pencil, muttering 'Bloody fool!', before giving them to Richard and Mary for making up and despatch.

I really enjoyed being one of three assistants making up deliveries for sending out to our branches of dispensing pharmacies. I loved weighing out orders of powders, flakes, seeds and crystals for pharmacy. Things like naptha flakes, sulphur, Epsom salts (my gran Peggy took them), some other vile-looking crystals called Epsom salts-cattle, as well as the more unpleasant jobs as derris dust (mask and goggles for that job which involved a shovel and a large sack), dried blood (horrible smell) and potassium nitrate. There was the counting out of large poppy heads. I used to shake them in their bag to see the tiny black seeds tumble out and I also loved cutting in to pieces the large slabs of cera flava.

I often lost myself in the wonderful and mysterious world of dry drugs a lot of which were stored down in the drugs basement, which we shared with the large carboys, etc. of the wet drugs department. As the youngest, I was the one who had to go down in the goods lift, which was operated by a continuous chain running from a hole in the lift cage floor to disappear through the roof, after closing the lift gates (I eventually fathomed out how to work the pull-chain control), with a wheeled flatbed trolley over to collect the stock. The cage would slowly descend into an atmosphere filled with the aromas of my stock! One wall was filled with large wooden drawers, on the end of which, the contents were listed on rather ornate gold-painted scrolls with black lettering. On being opened, each drawer would release the aromas, pleasant or otherwise, of the contents within.

My favourite substance above all others was 'cera flava' which, in layman's language meant yellow beeswax. I loved the rich smell of beeswax, and the shining, smooth texture between my fingers as I cut it and weighed it before putting it in the bag, which would then be checked and labelled upstairs by Mary and Richard before despatch.

Other drawers held unexpected things like black peppercorns called 'piper capsicum nigerum' and the dried giant poppy heads.

Apart from the drawers, '*my*' basement was a wondrous place with large bays holding bulk quantities of the dry drugs which were either loose in piles, at the bottom of the delivery chutes from the outside or stacked in large sacks. Some of the sacks were open and displaying the scoops used for filling my huge thick brown paper bags. There were also stored chemicals. Some of which were kept well away from each other, like sulphur, potassium nitrate and carbon, as these three are the the schoolboy ingredients for home-made fireworks so a fellow Yorkshireman by the name of Guy Fawkes could have answered the real reason for keeping them apart

I handled quite a lot of Glauber's salts, and I have a faint recollection of Mary telling me they were the largest crystals of Epsom salts. There was some dried plant like substance which was labelled 'Roots Quassia', and I believe they were steeped in boiling water and drunk like tea as an appetite stimulant. Other sacks near to them held flowers of camomile

D Day was a momentous happening, after nearly five years of war, but amazingly I didn't hear about it until 10 am, (I'd clocked on at 7.55 before any news had been anounced) when I had to go over to the works canteen, situated in the small block building away from the main factory, with the orders for tea and dripping toast for the other assistants. By this time, the whole place was agog with the news of the D-Day landings. The news bulletins were played over the radio system all day, a variation from '*Music While You Work*' and 'Housewives' Choice' that was usually played.

When asked if I remember 'D-Day'?, I always reply that 'of course I do' just as I remember every important happening that occurred during those horrible six *y*ears of my wartime childhood.

CHAPTER 10

A FAR DISTANT DRUM STARTS A-BEATING

DURING THE TERM OF my stay at Taylors' I only had one period of time off, and what a fuss Mr Simpson created before letting me have it! I wanted a Saturday morning off so that I could go with the army cadet band to Roundhay Park for a gala, or something similar, which was being held in the large arena there.

I was the bass drummer (in later years as a Guards drummer I would learn that the correct term was 'time beater') with the pipes and drums of the Second (Army Cadet) Battalion West Yorkshire Regiment. The First Battalion band was a very good bugle combination and sounded great. However the officer in charge of our band, Second Lieutenant Mullen, had been a piper in the pipes and drums of the Yorkshire Scottish Regimental Association (the 'Yorkshire Jocks') before the war and, in exchange for looking after their instruments, had got permission for our army cadet band to have temporary loan of the instruments until the members returned after the war. Mr Mullen's son was almost seventeen years of age, an excellent piper and our Pipe-Major, of course, besides being a teacher of the bagpipes like his dad.

As an aside, on some Saturday afternoons, using my precious time off from Taylors, I would go with my mum to Powolny's restaurant in Bond Street, Leeds, for the weekly tea dance which was held in the upstairs ballroom. The Powolny premises housed a large restaurant on the ground floor and this was a very large ornate dining room entered by glass doors from the richly carpeted entrance hall and foyer. Around the foyer were several alcoves, and it was the practice of mum to lead the way over to one which boasted a couple of easy chairs and a glass coffee table. Once settled there, she would order coffee and biscuits for the two of us, while we waited for the doors to open to the ballroom upstairs. There was a small stage in the foyer, which carried a grand piano and the music desks of a small string quartet, led by none other than Mr Mullen – the officer in charge of the pipe band who in addition to being an excellent piper, excelled only by his son, was a lovely violinist too.

Those tea dances were the start of my passion for ballroom dancing. Mum had taken ballet and ballroom dance lessons in her teenage years, and she taught me all the modern and 'old-time' techniques, twists and turns during those wonderful, music-filled late-Saturday afternoon tea dances in war-time Leeds. The dance band was an excellent six-piece outfit with a girl crooner, but the teas weren't up to much in my opinion. A pot of tea for two, two small Spam sandwiches, and two jam tarts made with pineapple conserve, would set mum back about 4 *shillings* (40p), which I considered daylight robbery! We had a jam factory in Leeds at that time called Moorhouse's Jams Ltd, the makers of 'Sonny Sunglow' Jams, and the pineapple conserve which was extremely popular with war time housewives wanting some decent jam to put on the table for their children. The conserve had never seen a pineapple of course, but thanks to the ingenuity of the lab at Moorhouses, it gave every indication of being a deliciously sweet preserve packed with that lovely tropical fruit, when in reality, of course, it was nothing more than cleverly chopped turnips, saccharine, pectin, and pineapple essence dispensed in a jam jar carrying a label displaying a large pineapple and the Sonny Sunglow motif of a little cherub wearing a baker's apron, trousers, and a tall baker's hat. All the kids in our house loved it anyway!

The Saturday of the gala at Roundhay Park promised to be sunny and dry and I set off, full of excited anticipation, with my bass-drum carried under my arm. I had spent quite a long time applying the black polish on my boots, and a fresh application of white 'blanco' on my belt and anklets. The White Horse of Hanover badge was a dazzle of gleaming silver in my forage cap, and I felt like the bee's knees!

Mr Mullen had agreed to let some girl dancers do a centre spot of Highland dancing during our display. The girls were Mr Mullen's niece and three of her friends, and this was to be their very first public performance as part of the band. They had been coming to band practice for a couple of months by then and were proficient in what they did. With their bonnets displaying eagle feathers, and their Montrose doublets and jabots, they looked really quite smart and would prove to be an asset to the band when we were performing. The plan was for them to march at the rear of the band, at the end of each of the four files, adding something a little different to the usual marching band line up. Unlike the pipers, they didn't wear sporrans with their kilts. The drummers didn't wear kilts either which I didn't mind as I liked our sharply creased battle-dress trousers, with the crafty few links of bicycle chain inside each leg to make the trousers drape nicely over our white webbing anklets.

The First Battalion Army Cadet Band had nothing like girl dancers to brighten up their own displays. However, they were a champion bugle band, and their Drum Major, Peter Horsfall, could leave our Drum Major standing when it came to staff drill and flourishes, for Peter was really outstanding! I didn't know it then of course, but fate had decreed that I would meet up with Peter again in our army life as, after failing to achieve his desire to enlist as a 'Boy' in the Royal Marines, Peter enlisted in the Coldstream Guards. When we met now and again over the years, I often tried to mention our cadet days, but he was climbing the promotion ladder and seemed to have left those memories behind?, but I never forgot my time in the army cadets myself. He had a really outstanding career, becoming in time a Regimental Sergeant Major. Before he retired, he rose to the rank of Major (QM), and then was employed for a few years as Superintendant Steward of the House of Lords, an aide to the stately person known as 'Black Rod'.

I was lucky living in Burley as I did, because I could catch a number 4 tram, which went all the way from Horsforth to the terminus at Roundhay Park. (Years later when I was on active service in Palestine, I would hear mention of the number 4 tram again from the mouth of a very attractive young female soldier in the Haganah. She had emigrated to Palestine from Leeds with her family at the end of the war).

I went through the bottom deck of the tram after boarding because I had my bass-drum with me. I had to put it under the stairs on the tram driver's platform, so it didn't present problems for other passengers who wished to put bags etc. under the stairs on the conductor's platform. As luck would have it, the tram driver that afternoon was a pal of my uncle Edgar, and although he couldn't get into the NFS with my uncle, they were still good pals and drinking buddies (when the pub had any beer!).

'Playing soldiers again, Rodney?' he said to me with a grin, knowing that he would get some retort from me - which he did, when I said, 'You won't be saying that when I get in the West Yorkshire's regimental band you know, Tracky!' And he just grinned back good-naturedly at me. It was touché really, because I know he didn't like being called 'Tracky' and I wouldn't dream of calling any other tram drivers by that nickname, which inferred they wouldn't know where to go if the tram car wasn't sitting on the tram tracks!

'I hope you get in, I really do, you know, but you are only fourteen aren't you?' Tracky asked me.

'I'll be fifteen in July!' I replied, but he just nodded.

'Well, fifteen in July, then, but I can't see any regiment taking young lads in until the war is over'

Then he helped me to stow my drum securely under his stairs. It looked big from the side, but it was a pipe-band bass drum, and only about ten inches deep from head to head, which made it very light, but with a mind of its own!

'Right, our kid' said Tracky, 'it'll be OK there. I'm having a break for half an hour at t'other end, so I might just come in and have a peep at these lasses that your uncle Edgar was telling me about OK?'

'I know what you'll be looking at Tracky' I said with a grin as I went back in the car, but he just winked and gave me a 'thumbs up'!

As the tram progressed along Kirkstall Road into the city centre, quite a few more lads from the band got on, and the sound gradually got louder as we all started telling jokes and speculating about the dancers' performance. The girls lived in the northern end of Leeds so they wouldn't be getting on this tram, so any premature flirting was out!

Disaster struck as the tram picked up speed at the top end of Briggate and swung round the bend. A lad sitting near the front had a view across the driver's platform, a view which was restricted from the rest of us by the anti shatter gauze netting stuck on every window.

'Hey up, Roddy!' he suddenly shouted, 't'bluddy bass drum's fallen off t' tram!' At this, I jumped to my feet and shoved my way to the front, where Tracky stood laughing his head off, as my flipping drum went bouncing, booming, and rolling down the slope of New York Road!

'OK, Roddy lad, I'll wait for you! don't worry!' (Good old Tracky!)

I jumped off his platform and was just in time to see a young girl stop the escapee, and, picking it up with both arms, was almost sprinting up to meet me.

'Thanks a lot,' I gasped, as she passed the instrument over. She waved her hand and told me it was no trouble.

'I'll be watching you in the arena later!' she called after me. Ah! She was well aware then of the trouble she had saved me from?

'Let's not have another accident, hey? - I'm not supposed to allow it, but you'd better just stand back here out of my way and keep a hand ready to catch that flipping wash tub!' Tracky said with a grin as I got back to the platform. With a clang, we were off again, a little bit behind time, but everyone having hysterics at my expense and cracking jokes about me having a female catcher taken on band strength, etc. All good-natured fun though, and I couldn't help joining in myself eventually.

The rest of the day went without a hitch. The girls were applauded, as they marched on, with their claymores at the carry, into the centre of the arena. With the Pipe Major playing, they went faultlessly through their routine sets of reel, strathspey, jig and with 'whoops' from the thousands on the arena banking, finished off with an enthusiastic 'broadswords'. What a terrific addition to our display, and Mr Mullen just grinned when all the band joined in with the clapping from where we were formed up, ready for the march off. The applause for us that day was ear-splitting as the 'big-wig' (whoever she was) took the salute.

Later that night, after my mum got in from the pub, I started chattering away ten to the dozen, but I soon discovered she had heard about the drum incident from Tracky in the pub, (blabbermouth!). But, when I started into my usual moaning about wishing I was in the forces 'proper' she held her hand up, and passed a newspaper to me saying, 'Open that and read the advert on page 18' (I think), so I took the paper. Turning to the page she mentioned, my eyes were drawn to a photo of a very young sailor under a headline which said something like, 'Is your son good enough to stand at his side?' The advert then went on to say that there were a few vacancies on the Training Ship 'Indefatigable' in North Wales, for 'sons of sailors, and other boys of good character'. Looking across at my mum, I said, 'Well, what am I supposed to be looking at?'

'I know it's not the army' she said with a sigh, 'but you keep nattering me about wanting to be a soldier like your dad, and this may not be the army, but apparently, you get signed on as an apprentice deck officer in the Merchant Navy, with a guarantee that you can go into the Royal Navy instead if you want to, when the time comes to leave. That's why that young boy there is in proper Royal Naval bell bottoms and blue-jean-collar, what do you think?' I started to become more interested and my Romany grandfather's genes started to bubble again as I looked beyond the confines of Leeds and the monotony of my job at Taylors'. I was looking instead towards a more interesting life in other climes and places! We discussed the possibilities far into the night, but when I eventually went to bed, I had agreed with Mum to apply to sit the entrance exam, which was to be held in a couple of weeks' time at a place called 'the Sailors' Home', Canning Place, in Liverpool. Liverpool? Crikey! I was going all the way across Lancashire for an exam and although I didn't realise it at the time, I had just taken the first tentative step towards a life that would see me in various uniformed services for the next forty years!

CHAPTER 11

CALLED TO THE SEA? - GOODBYE SAILOR!

WHEN THE DAY CAME for my tests at 'the Sailors' Home' in Liverpool my mum and my auntie Ethel (mum's sister) went with me on the train. It seemed a fairly long way and I remember going through that long dark tunnel under the Pennines into Lancashire, with a few stops on the way, including the big city of Manchester. I remember learning at school that the cotton industry was based there because cotton liked damp conditions. Everyone knew it was always raining in Manchester, that fact was often mentioned by the music teacher at 'Cockburn', my grammar school, whenever we had to sing 'Farewell Manchester.'

On arrival in Liverpool we walked through the streets to an address in Canning Place and arrived at 'the Sailors' Home', a multi storey brick built building which occupied a triangular corner in the area near the docks. After joining a group of about twenty other nervous-looking boys, I gave a tentative wave cheerio to my mum and auntie. The parents or guardians had been told to return at 3.30 p.m. to either pick us up again or, if we had been successful in all the tests, to say good bye to us before we left for the Training

Ship 'Indefatigable' in North Wales. Mum took my small suitcase of personal belongings with her for the time being.

Once our parents left the room a young Merchant Navy officer, with a blue stripe inlaid in the two gold bands at the bottom of his sleeve, called out our names then took us into a darkened room. Once we were all congregated together in the room, one by one, our names were called out and we had to sit at a table looking into a dark box amongst a bank of similar-looking 'pigeon holes.' As different pin pricks of light appeared at the back of the box we had to tell the officer conducting the test the number and position of the lights and their colours. That constituted of the whole of our eyesight test. We then had a very cursory medical check in a room with a doctor in a uniform that had red stripes laid in his gold bands. Red indicated a surgeon, and the blue in our conducting officer's rank markings were to show that he was connected with education.

Three boys were taken away to sit in a room for the rest of the day until the parents' party reassembled as they had failed the entry procedure at that point. The remainder of us were taken into a class room and told to write a short essay about something 'adventurous' – great! I wrote a short story about a young trapper living in the wilds of Canada. Talk about imagination! My efforts must have been satisfactory, because later that afternoon, I found myself with the half dozen or so boys bidding a fond farewell to our parents and me looking forward to a life wearing the bell-bottom trousers and blue-jean collar of a sailor, and of such is the stuff of dreams – or nightmares, as events would reveal! After a very tiring train and bus journey, we arrived in the early evening at our destination, the shore- based Training Ship 'Indefatigable'.

My visions of wearing the bell-bottom trousers and blue-jean collar were dashed when I found that we only wore that uniform for church parade on Sundays. This was when the entire ship's company marched about three miles to a little country church where most of the services were conducted in Welsh! The other occasion was when we went home on leave or when we went out to the nearby village on short 'shore leave' for a change of scenery. I could hardly wait for home leave to come, with its chance of my strolling down Kirkstall Road back home in Leeds, with Mavis Pickles hanging proudly on my arm as I flaunted the glittering gold letters of 'TS Indefatigable' on my cap tally for all to see!

At all other times however, we wore the navy-blue jumper jacket minus the blue-jean collar, navy-blue serge shorts and clogs of all things! I had been pestering my mum for a pair of clogs for ages back home in Leeds so I could be like most of the lads at my school, but she was adamant that I wore shoes. She had to unbend, however, when I joined the army cadets and the quarter-master gave me the necessary clothing coupons so she could produce the five shillings to purchase the obligatory part of my uniform. Wearing clogs at naval school was from dawn to dusk, with the footpaths in the camp resounding with the echoing clatter of wooden soles and iron rims.

The school was split up naval fashion into 'divisions,' but time has erased the memory of my division's name. We were housed in a long hut known as a mess deck. There were about fifty two-tiered bunks stretching length wise along the sides of the building, while along the other wall was a row of wooden lockers for our belongings. Our bell-bottom trousers were always laid under the bottom blanket in our bunk, with them folded in such a way as to produce the seven rows of horizontal 'seven-seas' creases running down their length, while we slept on them. They had no fly on them, so when needed, we had to drop the front flap, which was fastened by two buttons, one on each corner.

My dreams of life in the Navy started to wear thin after the first few early shouts of 'hands off your cocks - put on your socks!' from a beefy-faced old bo'sun at the ungodly hour of 5.30 am! Up to that time I had not been used to being exposed to the obscenities as issued constantly from that evil individual's mouth. I remember the quick slap across my face and the lecture I got from Mum one day when I followed the stupid urging from a gang of big girls playing outside our house. 'Dare you to go in and ask your mum what this means!' said one of the girls, leaning and whispering something unmentionable in my ear!

After lining up outside our mess decks, we then spent about an hour and a half scrubbing the mess deck floors, trestle tables etc and performing our morning ablutions before being marched to breakfast by our boy Petty Officer. He wore a badge on his arm consisting of crossed anchors crowned with an embroidered figure of a Liver bird, because of the school's affiliation to the city of Liverpool and the school being based on a wooden ship afloat on the River Mersey there in pre-war days. I liked him; he was one of the few friendly ones I met in that dreary establishment, and I bet he made a great skipper one day.

The ship's company was divided in to two halves, or 'watches', for routines. The 'starboard watch' would spend three months doing naval training and classroom education while the 'port watch' would learn more of the general ship's routine. This included cleaning duties, working in the galley, duty bugle duties (if they were able) and the incessant work painting the premises which never ended, – as it seems would be the routine all the time at sea. I remembered those painting routines in the future when I saw the Forth Bridge which, until recently, had to have the same never ending paint applications, I believe.

I was still only fourteen years old and I became terribly homesick during my first few months at the school. The whole experience of a sailor's life palled rapidly, beginning with the constant punishing sessions when we had to pull on the heavy oars of a 'whaling' boat around a nearby lake for a few hours. This resulted in blistered palms, which never seemed to fade. I was given to walking miserably on my own around the school football pitch, gazing wistfully at the distant blue and green mountains while yearning to be beyond them and back home again.

Things came to a head for me on my fifteenth birthday, when I was made to 'ride the crow's nest' which was made from about six of the small lockers piled on top of each other. After being forced to climb to the top one, I had to cling to it while the stack was rocked to and fro until the pile collapsed, with me trusting the open arms held out reassuringly beneath me – which were then closed as I fell heavily to the ground. I was then held down by some of the other boys while my shorts were pulled down. I felt the scrape of a razor, followed by a liberal application of black boot polish and the slap of a sheet of newspaper on my nether regions, after which my attackers dispersed, leaving me to pull up my shorts and run, wailing, out to the solitude of the football field. That was enough, and I poured out my troubles in a letter home to my gran Peggy.

A week later I was summoned to the skipper's office one day to be greeted by the wonderful sight of my gran Peg, my mum, and my auntie Dolly, sitting in a group facing the skipper's desk in silence. There followed a discussion between Gran and the skipper where she demanded that I be allowed to accompany my visitors 'ashore' for a while. After donning my bell-bottoms and blue-jean collar, I was taken by them to a small farm house on the outskirts of the nearby village of Clawdd Newydd. We had a wonderful ham-and-egg tea, then lingered for about an hour while I told them of everything that had gone on during my time at the school. This included the bo'sun's practice of intercepting any parcels arriving by post for the boys and opening them to see if any cigarettes were enclosed. If he found any, he would then confiscate them to his own pockets, as no boys were allowed to smoke, of course, but it was theft all the same.

I didn't smoke, but I heard of two boys who had purchased a packet of five Woodbine one day from the village shop only to be met at the ship's gate on their return by the bo'sun, who made them produce their purchase following a telephone call he had received from that 'kindly' Welsh lady shopkeeper!

After a while, my mum, gran and auntie agreed that it was not a suitable place for me and I was to be removed from the training ship immediately. It was with a light step I returned to the school with them for what was to be a long heated exchange of words between Gran and the skipper, after which she produced two £5 notes (not a small amount at that time) to cancel my indentures as a Merchant Navy cadet officer. I was then taken by the bo'sun to collect the brown paper parcel from the ship's stores which held my plain clothes ready for the time when I would have taken them back home when

I went on leave, leaving them at home. There was a long, blistering, and obscene commentary from the bo'sun as I changed hurriedly out of my uniform, which I then dumped on the bed.

After getting dressed, I had to make my way out between the two lines of boys on either side of the mess deck, there as a result of a hurried muster. At the bo'sun's command, they commenced to batter me about the shoulders with rolled-up and knotted towels to the accompaniment of their shouts of 'You weed! You're a bloody weed!' (with perhaps a smattering of more colourful language in amongst the chants). None shouted louder than that flipping evil old bo'sun!

I escaped from that place with a new determination, that come what may, a sailor's life was most definitely not for me. I cemented that vow on my return home, with another visit to the army recruiting office in Leeds to be met again by the RQMS with 'O bloody 'ell, not you again lad!' Meanwhile, Mavis Pickles dumped me like a hot potato when she realised that I had left the bell-bottom trousers, blue-Jean collar and gold- lettered cap tally back in Wales!

On my return home, I got a job as a trainee cobbler, but I wasn't the flavour of the month after doing a 'complete sole and heel' of his son's shoes as a test, only for the soles to start gaping at school due to my using the wrong size of rivets (the name given to shoemakers' nails). It took me quite a while to redeem myself after that gaffe!

I resumed making occasional visits to the army recruiting office in Leeds, whenever I got a chance, as I tried to join the West Yorkshire regiment as a junior musician. I was trying to follow in the footsteps of a friend of mine, Jack Foster, who had been lucky enough to be accepted into the regiment even though it was still war time. I always got the same reception from the RQMS in the recruiting office: 'I keep telling you son there will be no more boys accepted by the army until after the war, so bugger off like a good lad!' So, I had to satisfy my military ambitions for the time being by re-joining the army cadets and once again taking on the position of bass-drummer in the pipe band.

On the 7th of May came the surrender of the German forces. A cease fire was put in place to save lives until the official end of the war in Europe the following day on the 8th of May, a day full of celebrating to be called VE Day. The Japanese were still clinging on in Burma and other places in the Far East though. There was a huge street party in our neighbourhood, with sandwiches, tea, pop, music, and games. I remember the thrill of winning a three-legged race with a girl of our street and getting a rare orange each for our efforts, I hadn't had an orange for years! The night sky was rosy red with the reflected glow from thousands of bonfires as the country celebrated VE Day, and I tagged along with a gang of my teenage friends as we joined in the singing and dancing in a variety of locations. What a great night that was, but my dad was still with the army in Italy and wouldn't be returning home for a few more weeks to come.

Eventually the war in the east ended with the dropping of atom bombs on Hiroshima and Nagasaki in Japan. This brought the Japanese High Command to surrender at last, so we had another celebration in August - VJ Day. In early September, my dad arrived back home on 'demob' from the army and returned to civilian life with his family. However, his little family unit was to be altered once again when I called in to the army recruiting office to be told that the Brigade of Foot Guards was now returning to its peace time establishment. This meant therefore they were now accepting the enlistment of boys over the age of fourteen to serve in one of the five regiments of Foot Guards.

When I asked the recruiting RQMS if that included the Coldstream Guards, the regiment of Guards much favoured by Yorkshiremen, he replied 'Well, you will have to enlist first and see where you are posted to, OK?' It certainly was OK by me, and I scampered most of the way back home to tell my news excitedly to my mum and dad. I expected my dad to give me a proud hug, but he wasn't quite as pleased as I'd expected!

'Don't be such a bloody little fool.' He told me, 'You just get me home after nearly six years, and now you want to clear off to the blasted army in my place? Well, you're *not* going, so you can forget it!' I received this outburst with horror and tears of disappointment, and I cried most of that night in to my pillow. However, I was met next morning by my mum telling me, 'Me and your dad have been having another think, and if you are really determined to join the Guards, we'll let you go, but no repeat of the naval school business, mind!' I almost jumped for joy, though all I got was 'Humph!' from my dad when I threw my arms round his shoulders as he dipped a bread 'soldier' in his boiled egg. We still had plenty of these from our hens for the time being.

Weeks of having the necessary medical examinations by the army recruiting team doctors followed. To this day I have never figured out what a doctor expected to discover by being up, close and personal in every pit and bit of a sixteen-years-old boy as the lad was bent over, upwards, backwards, forwards!

Eventually, just a couple of months after the end of my wartime years living in the home front shadows, I emerged on Friday the 12th of October 1945, sitting on a train bound for London, after swearing to serve His Majesty King George VI, his heirs, and successors, clutching my travel warrant and my enlistment form. On arrival in the huge, bustling city of London and after asking for directions (when I managed to get one of the scurrying hordes of passers-by to pause for a few moments), I managed to get from King's Cross Station to London Bridge Station, where I boarded a Southern Railway train bound for Caterham and my recruit training at the Guards Depot as an enlisted 'Boy Soldier'. It was not however to be in the Coldstream Guards as I had wanted at first, but infact in the Welsh Guards for some reason. I must say that I was feeling a bit apprehensive when I finally boarded a bus at Caterham Station for the climb up Caterham Hill and . . . my destiny? Well, perhaps so, but that had yet to be revealed!

Rod's birthplace, Craven Street, Leeds.

Rod's baptism with Auntie Rhoda, August 1929.

Rod at six months.

With my dad and his van, 1932.

After a stay in hospital with diptheria, 1934.

As a pageboy in 1935 with Kathleen. (I thought I'd married her!)

Rod when a WWII evacuee, October 1939.

Army Cadet Force at the age of 13, 1942.

My first photograph as a boy in the Welsh Guards, 1945.

Home on leave - with my gran Peg, Leeds, 1947.

A Grenadier at last! January 1947.

With the Grenadier Guards Corps of Drums
in 1947. (Rod on cymbals!)

Corps of Drums sailing to Egypt, March 1948.

Duty bugler, August 1948, Libya.

With my dear buddy Les, in Egypt, 1948. He dared
me to wear that blinkin' fez for the photo!

Corps of Drums Corporal-in-waiting, September 1949, Libya.

As a Drum Major in the Grenadier Guards, wearing State Dress during the Queen's Birthday Parade (Trooping the Colour).

As Drum Major wearing State Dress.

In Guard Order.

As the Drum Major of the West Riding County Fire Service Band.

Instructor at the West Riding County Fire Service training school.

At my desk in the Grampian Fire Brigade Training School.

Taking a breather during a Fire Service officers' mess dinner.

Receiving my plaque upon my retirement from the
Fire Service College, Moreton-in-Marsh 1984.

CHAPTER 12

A BOY SOLDIER OF THE KING- PART 1

THE RED DOUBLE-DECKER BUS was obviously of pre-war vintage, and seemed to be making slow progress up Caterham Hill, probably as a result of my own wishful thinking. I took a quick glance towards the luggage rack and my battered little suitcase (packed so lovingly by my mum the previous evening with socks, sighs and solemn warnings) and yes, it was still there.

A few weeks after my soldier dad arrived home on demob (he had been fighting with the Fifth Army in North Africa and Italy) he finally gave in to my pleadings and gave parental consent for me to take advantage of the news that the Brigade of Guards was now reintroducing the peacetime policy of allowing the enlistment of 'Boy' soldiers to its exclusive ranks. As a Yorkshire lad I had been keen to join the Coldstream Guards. So, it has remained a mystery to this old Grenadier, how then, on the twelfth day of October 1945, – I found myself standing in front of the recruiting officer in Leeds holding the Bible in my right hand and taking a solemn oath to defend His Sovereign Majesty King George the Sixth, his heirs, and successors as a recruit in the ranks of . . . the Welsh Guards! How that came about I will never know. Probably someone balancing the books?

After duly signing on the dotted line I made my way to Leeds Central Station, clutching a travel warrant, for my bone-rattling journey by steam locomotive to London and then to the Guards Depot at Caterham in Surrey. Part of my journey, during this long wearisome day, entailed finding myself in London for the first time in my young life and encountering the faceless hurrying hordes of this great city, which one day I would learn to love.

My reverie was suddenly shattered by the friendly clippie's shout of 'Here we are, me ducks – the Guards Depot. But mind you, don't go in the wrong gate. The uvver place next door's a loony bin!' So, I duly found myself deposited with my meagre belongings on the pavement, gazing wistfully after the cocooned warmth of the disappearing bus and the pretty waving girl on the platform. I never saw her again unfortunately as she had chatted encouragingly on and off during my trip from Caterham Station to the Depot.

'Aye! Tak a last wee look, laddie, then let's be having you in here'. I turned with a start towards the source of this remark and almost flattened my nose on a gaily coloured band of medal ribbons sitting on a sea of khaki, which was on the chest of the tallest man I had ever seen. My gaze seemed to climb for ever until I met two kindly but quizzical blue eyes peering down at me from the underside of a 'rib-stitched' peak cap. At the top of each shoulder was a blue designation with the words *ScotsGuards* picked out in gold letters.

My attention was distracted for a moment by the sight of a boy much the same age as myself (or so I thought) in the background who seemed to be grinning in a friendly manner at me. I will always remember he had a tooth missing from the upper row and that he was wearing a soft-looking khaki cap with a minute gleaming silver star set in the front and, for some reason, he was leaning on a walking stick. As soon as our eyes met, however, the young mouth snapped shut – I swear I heard the click! Drawing himself up to his full height he screamed out in a juvenile, albeit refined voice, 'Carry on, Sergeant!' This was my first encounter with a Guards officer, and I learned later that he was about twenty years of age and not long out of Sandhurst as an ensign. I was to discover that the walking stick carried by that young officer is a vital piece of parade equipment for Guards officers (except when wearing ceremonial dress) and it is more correctly referred to as an 'ash plant' for officers in the Irish Guards a 'blackthorn'. While the Sergeant of the barrack guard questioned my unseemly arrival on a Friday (a 'no intake' day), I noticed the reassuring outlines of the church opposite the guard room, and my sinking spirits took a slight uplift as I comforted myself with the thought that my God had not forsaken me! In later days I was to spend quite a few soul-searching hours in that beautiful Guards Chapel at Caterham. I was confirmed there the following year by the Bishop of Woolwich.

Directly in front of the church wall was a sentry box painted with the blue-red-blue stripes of the Household Brigade, and this was the back cloth for a young soldier of the Irish Guards standing rigidly 'at ease' (I had learned a bit about drill in the Army Cadet force) with a .303 Lee Enfield rifle at an angle between his right hand and the asphalt roadway. Equally motionless in front of the guard room door was another Irish Guardsman minus rifle, who suddenly slammed both boots together and seemed to jump about a foot in the air as he flew in to the guardroom in response to the Sergeant's scream of 'Picqet sentry!' After a long string of unintelligible commands to the quaking young soldier, the Sergeant then let forth another screech, which embraced the pair of us, and off we shot down a seemingly endless driveway past vast expanses of drill grounds, barrack blocks and tear-stained windows, until we arrived at the small building which was the 'receiving room' – and where I was to spend my first night in the army.

A waxy museum smell enveloped us as we entered the small four-roomed block and stood in the glow thrown out by a pot-bellied stove, which reflected in the highly polished floor and the glass of the many group photographs which covered the walls. Some of the photographs were obviously dated back to the time of the Boer War, showing the Battles of Modder River, Ladysmith and the like, as some of the groups were wearing white shell jackets and pillbox caps (the sailor-type 'Broderick' cap, a forage style cap with no peak, was a much later version of this headgear). Sad faces, many adorned with waxed 'Guardee' moustaches, gazed at me vaguely over the years, and I started to feel the first stirrings of a chilly apprehension.

My companion opened his mouth to bellow 'New recruit for you, Trained Soldier!' Giving me a broad wink, he whispered, in a broad scouse accent, 'Pity you couldn't get in the Micks, lad' and scurried away through the beckoning doorway amid a decreasing clatter of his heel irons and studs. I was left to gaze in fascination at a seemingly ancient old man who, with a bamboo swagger cane under his arm, was approaching me from the shadows of his lair under the stairs. He sported no chevrons of rank, but, at the bottom of his left sleeve was a row of inverted service chevrons and two gold wound stripes. On his right upper sleeve was a gleaming brass star within a circlet bearing the words 'Trained Soldier'.

I discovered later that there was one of these veterans attached to each squad, and as disciplinarians in their own right, they were responsible to the squad instructors for barrack room discipline and for imparting those many aspects of army 'know- how' which can only come from a font of experience recalled while sat round in those magic moments of chatting to his recruits in the atmosphere of the barrack room. At the top of each sleeve he displayed the red-and-white designations of the Coldstream Guards, and reposing on his head was a short-peaked khaki cap, on the front of which twinkled a brass replica of the star of 'The Order Of The Garter' – the badge of the Coldstreamers.

'Not only do they send me a recruit on a 'no intake' day – but it has to be a flipping kid for me to baby sit!' he muttered. Then, seeing the first slight tremble of a previously stiff upper lip, his manner softened as he said, 'Never mind me, son. I was a drummer boy myself back in the twenties. You'll be OK once you get with your future squad mates tomorrow'. This was my first clue, had I noticed it at that time, that my future was to be as a member of a Corps of Drums and *not*, as I had been expecting, learning to play some exotic instrument with a Guards band and performing on the BBC in things such as '*Music While You Work*' radio programmes. A certain recruiter in Leeds would have some explaining to do if I ever got the chance to challenge him about his promises of musical glory!

After issuing me with a white china pint mug, knife, fork and spoon (ever after to be referred to as 'eating irons') he led the way to an upstairs room and a number of fold-up beds, each with a set of three-piece small mattresses known as 'biscuits'. Wherever he is now, that craggy-faced man with a heart of gold, I hope he had a long and happy retirement and the happiness that was his due, for he displayed a wealth of human understanding that night to a young homesick boy who was starting to have second thoughts about the challenge of a soldier's life. He seemed ancient to me at the time, but he was probably only in his mid thirties!

Sleep eluded me for quite a while after I had tried to get comfortable in the hairy warmth of the coarse blankets. ('No sheets in the Guards, son - they all get allocated to the 'Brylcreem Boys' in the RAF!') Every time I swallowed the homesick lump in my throat and started to doze off, it seemed there was some devilish plot conspired to send a bugler to issue a brazen taunt under the window, only ceasing at about 10.30 p.m. with 'Lights Out'. At odd intervals thereafter, the silence was broken by the double bell chimes of the Guards Depot clock - two at quarter past the hour, four at half past, and so on. Faint memories were brought back to me of my previous year at naval school in Wales as the familiar bells chimed throughout the night. How many thousands of Guardsmen must have cursed those all-pervading chimes over the years but, in other less secure circumstances, would have given all they possessed at that time to be back within range of the sounds of the Guards 'family clock'?

My awakening on my first full day in the army was not as harsh as others during the following weeks. This was thanks to the understanding of the Trained Soldier, who knew what the future held for an enlisted boy in the Guards, as he led me through the early morning routine at a fairly leisurely pace.

Taking me over to a huge dining hall filled with hundreds of shaven-headed young men who seemed intent on teasing me with calls of 'You'll be sorry!', my mentor helped me to collect some hot metal containers and a galvanised bucket half-full of some vicious-looking tea. After picking up some thick slices of bread from a tea chest at the end of a trestle table, on which stood a contraption like a sausage machine which dispensed little serrated discs of margarine, we went back to his block for a leisurely Saturday breakfast, accompanied by a few more words of wisdom from him. After the previous six years of wartime rationing, and a scarcity of certain items of food, that first breakfast in the army seemed like a feast. We must have had double rations and I tucked in with gusto to make up for all those recent skimpy school-day breakfasts enforced by the war. I did not even pause to marvel that for the first time in my life I was being introduced to the peculiarities and ingenuity of army chefs as they catered for the demands of hungry, hard-pushed soldiers. Who ever heard of braised liver and mashed potatoes for breakfast? It was delicious, and I have never forgotten either the taste or the company of that Trained Soldier (or TS as we knew him).

All good things must come to an end, however. After helping me to return our utensils and plates back to the mess room, he started to get me ready to move out of the reception room. It seemed that the time had come for me to 'gird my loins' and prepare to meet my future companions. Picking up my suitcase I found myself scurrying after the TS. He seemed to have regained his mantle of authority as he suddenly barked over his shoulder, 'Come on, lad – move yourself!' There had been a stray 'doodlebug' bomb the previous year which had found its way to the depot and demolished part of one of the barrack-blocks. All of the barrack-blocks were named after famous Generals. It transpired that I was to be accommodated during my 'unsquadded' week in Roberts Block, which was the block hit by the the 'doodlebug'. I was staying within the part of the building that had survived, the demolished section having been cleared and the space turned into a small drill ground. Standing in the entrance of the block was the man who was to be my Trained

Soldier – Guardsman 'Dusty' Smith of the Grenadier Guards. Like my companion, I noticed that he too had a couple of wound stripes at the bottom of his left sleeve, and I wondered 'was this the prerequisite of being a Trained Soldier at the Guards Depot?' After speaking for a while to my previous companion Dusty turned, and with a brief smile, crooked a beckoning finger at me as I followed him in to the block to meet my future squad companions and destiny!

As we entered the block, my new Trained Soldier (TS), Dusty, turned around and said 'Don't get too cosy in here, because as soon as the squad is up to full strength next weekend, we will be moving to one of those huts over there' as he pointed through the doorway in the direction of the roadway to where six barrack-huts stood on the edge of a small football pitch. We climbed a dog-legged stone staircase to the first floor, which was also (unusual for the Depot barrack-blocks) the top floor. I noticed that the long barrack-room to my left was empty except for about a dozen beds. Over each one was a wall-mounted wooden rack, with about three pegs on the underneath.

Our destination was through the closed door at the end of the landing to our left, past an open doorway through which I could see a row of washbasins ('only *one* tap over each one? – *Funny*' I thought) and one slate urinal reminiscent of those in my old school playground back home.

'Don't use that urinal during the day, lad it's only for night-time use - that's why we call them 'night-lines' my TS said, as he saw me looking at them, 'You must use the latrines by 'K' company office at any other time, got it?' It transpired that the Boys' squads, like the one I was to join, were called 'Brigade Squads' as each contained boys from all five regiments of Foot Guards. They were attached to 'K' Company Scots Guards for all administration which is why we had a Scots Guards 'Superintendant Sergeant.'

As the TS opened the door to the remaining room, I noticed to my surprise that most of the beds were empty except for those being used by the other occupants of the room, and there were only three of those!

'This is another newcomer lads. That's why I had you making up that other bed. Look after him and I'll see you tomorrow.' Away he went, back down the stairs and along the road somewhere. The three other boys came over to greet me and to make themselves known. They were Bob from Lancaster, who was in the Scots Guards, George from Carlisle, and Ray from Orpington, who were both in the Welsh Guards like myself.

There were no Welsh Guards Boys in the two senior squads, which had been training for a couple of weeks, so as strange as it seems, the first three Boys to enlist into the Welsh Guards regiment after WWII were all English! Ray (later to be dubbed 'Zulu' by all who knew him) was particularly friendly towards me and helped me a lot during that first time-wasting weekend. We remained friends long after I had transferred to the Grenadier Guards and through into later life, until his untimely passing in 2002 at his home in Torquay. I was amused at first by his southern accent, which took a while to get used to, but he was a great chum and told a lot of schoolboy jokes which had us all giggling. I started to cheer up a lot as the day went on and after coming back from our dinner, we all sat on the grass to watch a football match being played between two Scots Guards recruit squads, egged on by their Trained Soldiers. Life in the army was not looking too bad after all! I felt a bit out of place during that Saturday and Sunday dressed in my sports coat, flannels, and my rather grubby striped shirt (which was open at the neck) while my three companions were dressed in khaki-greenish canvas battledress blouses and trousers (which I learned were called 'denims') and stiff khaki serge berets with their regimental badges over the left eye. They also wore brown canvas gym shoes instead of boots (apparently this was OK at odd times when not actually marching about), and all three seemed completely at ease in their recently issued working garb. Apparently I would be getting my 'stuff' on Monday, and I could not wait to blend in with everyone else.

The Trained Soldier came in to see us on Sunday morning to check that we were up. After about half an hour of telling us bits of information about our future weeks ahead, he said 'There will be quite a lot of new lads coming to join you over the next few days, so enjoy your space while you can!' After a few more "do's and don'ts", he left us to our own devices for the rest of the day.

On Sunday afternoon, my new buddies took me with them on a tour round the Depot so I could find out more about where everything was. The Barracks part of the pre-war Guards Depot had not been big enough to accommodate the thousands of recruits signing up to serve in the five regiments on active service in the recent war. The necessary added living space sprawled towards the village of Coulsdon, in a huge encampment of single-storey Barrack huts, which we came to know as 'Tin Town'.

There was a roadway running through part of it that was called 'The Grove' so all the surrounding area was referred to as 'Grove Lines'. There was also a large cookhouse and mess room (which we used), a big NAAFI canteen (to cater for the overflow from the Barrack's NAAFI), a Gymnasium, and oddly enough, also a Pub! The camp had spread to such an extent that it was forced to embrace the nearest pub, – 'The Fox'. Over the next few years, as the Guards depot shrank back down to a pre-war size and things started to settle again, 'Tin Town' and the Grove Lines would disappear and the villagers of Coulsdon could reclaim 'The Fox' as their own again. As we were attached to 'K' Company Scots Guards, we were classed as being in the Grove Lines, and we were to see very little of the Barracks proper except when on Church parade or going up to the Gym or the old-fashioned swimming baths.

All our foot drill instruction was done on the small parade ground formed by the cleared area left by the demolition of the bomb-damaged part of Roberts Block.

My head was spinning with all the new information, and I was quite a while drifting off to sleep on Sunday night, knowing that a lot more changes were coming my way on Monday morning in the form of kit and uniform issues and another medical examination. It seemed that I had to see the depot Medical Officer (MO) soon because of the depot's need to satisfy the rigid fitness requirements of the Brigade of Guards, as opposed to the 'If they are breathing they are OK' approach at the recruiting offices (a slight exaggeration there, of course!). It was to be a few days later, though, before I was to meet the Medical Officer.

On Monday morning I was taken to the quartermaster's stores to be issued with my uniform and equipment, and what a bewildering half hour that was! After having a kit bag thrust over the counter at me by the store-man who was assisted by my TS, I had a vast selection of uniform clothing, underwear (intended for an Eskimo), webbing equipment, and other smaller items, all virtually thrown at me to be either stuffed in to the big kit bag or piled up for carrying. There was one slightly puzzling piece of small kit passed to me called a 'razor-3 piece-GS – soldiers.' (Everyone spoke back to front in that Aladdin's cave.) When the TS explained what it was, I piped up with 'But - I don't shave, Trained Soldier' The TS gave me a look of disdain as he replied, – 'You do now lad, get that flipping bum-fluff off your chin!'

When we got back to the barrack-room, I was told to spend the rest of the day stencilling my regimental number (2741341) with white or black paint on all my clothing and equipment or stamp it on hard items such as brushes and button stick with a set of metal punches and a hammer. My two battledress blouses had been dropped off at the tailors' shop to have the black-and-white shoulder designations sewn on. I have mentioned the underwear, it was a joke! We had two pairs of long baggy woollen under-drawers with rubber buttons, and a pair of woollen long johns! (I was only sixteen for heaven's sake!) At the waist bands were loops to help the garments to be hoisted up by the huge broad white braces we all wore. The woollen vests were to match and had three rubber buttons at the neck opening.

Two items of my clothing were disappointing. The lovely, natural, light-coloured cap strap was to be worked at with Kiwi dark tan shoe polish, the TS said, 'Until it looks like the jacket of a flipping horse chestnut, got it?' The other disappointment was the huge peak on my khaki service-dress cap. We were told that the large peaks were the hallmark of a recruit Guardsman, and they would not be cut until we left the depot on the conclusion of our basic training to become members of our respective 'Training Battalions'. Even when they were tailored by the battalion tailors' shop, the peaks were only shortened, and they stuck out slightly.

'Your long-peaked caps' the TS said, with a smirk, 'are to keep the sun out of your eyes, and make you hold your head erect!' Some Guardsmen, anxious to impress girls and relatives while on leave, would cut the stitching at the side of the peak and push it up and inwards so that it laid flat against their forehead. This practice was an offence against military discipline and, if charged with 'slashing' his peak ('altering the design'), the offender could expect to receive about seven days CB (confined to barracks). Now, many years later as I look around, it seems that these 'illegal' peaks are now the 'norm' throughout The Household Division, and are even worn tiny and flat on the forehead by Senior Warrant Officers – the very first ones in my young days to spot a 'floating peak' from afar. The unlucky offender would then receive a violent 'ear-bashing' before being placed in open arrest to face his company commander the next day (or the Adjutant, in the case of Drummers).

The rest of our first week was spent blancoing our web equipment and polishing all our brasswork and badges with 'Bluebell' Metal Polish (after first smoothing all the surfaces with Bath Brick). We were taught how to square off all our large and small packs and display them above our beds for the benefit of uniformity. When they were all lined up on the shelves with brass buckles sparkling, even our very particular TS started to be more affable at times!

Our two pairs of boots, complete with heel and toe plates, and the regulation thirteen studs on each sole (these plates and studs had to be burnished!) came straight from the manufacturers with pimply surfaces. These then had to be 'boned' flat with a tooth brush handle until all the pimples disappeared to leave a smooth surface which then had to be 'worshipped' for hours with black Kiwi Black boot Polish and thousands of the proverbial 'spit-and-polish' small circles, applied with a finger-end and a yellow duster. The Trained Soldier would not be satisfied until they looked like black glass. (The result of many hours of determination and sweat!)

Meanwhile our squad numbers were increasing, with the daily arrivals of other Boys destined for all five regiments. There were to be ten Welsh Guards Boys in my squad eventually, with the other seven of them coming from South Wales (and what a mixed bunch they were to prove themselves to be later on!).

And so that week dragged on, with the days of our 'unsquadded' status finally coming to an end of the following Sunday. (Gosh! Was it only just over a week since I stepped off that bus?). Our Trained Soldier and Sergeant Smith of the Welsh Guards (our squad instructor, no relation to the TS), informed us that the following day we were to vacate the 'comforts' of Roberts Block and move across to one of 'K' Company's barrack- huts to become a squad at last. We were now to commence our training!

All during the day of Monday, 22nd October 1945 (the date is burned into my memory), we trudged backwards and forwards from Roberts Block to our new billet in the 'K' Company huts, one of about six around the perimeter of the Grove Lines football field. When we entered the hut for the first time, I was aware of the length of what appeared to be a big 'Wolf Scouts' hut' with a glaring-white scrubbed wooden floor and lots of windows all sparkling like diamonds! Two big solid-fuel stoves stood, like blackleaded dustbins, waiting for their first meals of glowing coke when we eventually got settled in. I noticed a large square board up in the roof joists, and from the meshed centre of this, there was drifting the muted strains of a girl crooner with orchestral backing warbling the latest 'hit' of that time . . . 'Symphony.'

I suppose we did break off from our labours to be fed, but all I can remember is the shock of realising that I was going to be living in this 'shed' with all my squad companions for the rest of my recruit training and the prospect was a little daunting. We were allocated our bed-spaces by the Trained Soldier, much to the chagrin of one or two boys who were rapidly emerging as the 'bully boys' of the squad. They had charged straight over to the hut corner to claim 'prime' spots, only to be promptly turfed out.

'You can flipping well come out of there, that corner is reserved for me!' bellowed the TS. That was them told! I noticed that there was a marked absence of mattresses or 'biscuits' on the bare bed springs, but in the afternoon I realised why as we were marched over to a large barn like structure filled to the eaves with bales of straw, where we were each issued with large man-sized canvas bags, open at one end and fitted with tapes also.

'Fill your bags with straw, lads, and be careful, the way you pack them will decide how well you sleep at night, because these are your mattresses. They are called 'palliasses', but there is nothing friendly about these flipping donkeys!' It was quite funny hearing this for the first time, we all giggled dutifully, but how many times did he repeat this old chestnut I wonder?

We were still expected to fold our battledress trousers and blouses, plus our greatcoats under our blanket for pressing while we slept, and wonder of wonders . . . it worked! The process called for us to brush up and down each garment pleat with copious amounts of water with our shaving brushes, holding the completed folds together with such aids as our forks and button sticks. The heat of our sleeping bodies on the top of each 'pile' would dry the damp garments and set the creases. There was not the luxury of steam irons (or even ordinary flat irons) in those early days however our immaculately creased trousers and blouse sleeves would not have suggested any deficiencies in that area, for they were as sharply defined as any depot squad instructor could desire.

After the evening tea meal, dressed in our denim trousers and khaki shirts, we had a nightly period of instruction in our barrack-hut which included a procedure known as 'Shining Parade'. For this period, we each had one blanket spread out on the palliasse tucked in with 'hospital corners' (we hoped!), and over this expanse, we spread our ground sheet. In front of the bed stood our kit bag, folded over at the top to reveal our name and regimental number. Armed with all our cleaning materials and our uniform articles requiring attention, we then sat astride our beds with braces slipped down and hanging down each side of our body (why?). Using the same white one-pint china mug that we used at meal times, but now filled with water, we started the two-hour task of polishing brasses and blancoing web equipment (using our shaving brushes!). During this monotonous ordeal, the TS would strut up and down the length of the billet while asking questions on regimental history and battle honours, etc. whilst slapping the sides of his legs with his swagger cane. We didn't realise at the time of course, but one of the benefits of being in a brigade squad was that these sessions gave us a good grounding in the history, customs, and battle honours of all five regiments in the Household Brigade and *not* just our own, as prevailed in the mens' regimental squads. (I believe they did touch lightly on the regiments other than their own).

At the end of our first day in the new billet we had our first couple of hours 'exposure' to our squad instructor, Sergeant Smith of the Welsh Guards, a very smart man with sandy hair and a clipped gingerish moustache. He told us quite a bit about his background before he was called up for war service, and a lot more about his travels with his Welsh Guards battalion during the recent conflict.

At one point he told us a few things also about our TS which the man would not have revealed himself. Indicating the wound stripes on the left sleeve of the TS, he asked him to roll up his trousers to reveal some ugly scars on both legs – reminders of the injuries he had sustained while on active service with the Grenadiers. Although both of our guardians were strict disciplinarians and dedicated to the 'nth degree' there were odd moments during those evenings in the hut, when each of them would mention his 'release group' number with a certain amount of longing evident in the way they spoke of them. During the time of National Service, each new entrant to the army was allocated a release group number. This number indicated the order in which a Solider could expect to leave the colours to join the reserve. I had a release group too, but when I showed it to the TS (it was shown in the front of each man's AB64 pay book) he pointed out that the number 72 (appertaining to my release group), also had the letters *DR* after it. This translated to indicate 'deferred regular', in other words I had to 'soldier on' when number 72 came up.

At one point during that first evening, the door opened, and Sergeant Smith barked out, 'Squad shun! – Sit up straight' The new arrival was a rugged faced man in a khaki greatcoat, wearing one of those caps which I yearned to wear. (Namely a cap with a peak covered with rows of stitching and which seemed to have a front which towered up for ever!) He had three chevrons on each sleeve, sported the silver 'Order of the Thistle' badge of a Scots Guards full Sergeant and carried a pace stick under his arm. He promptly told us to sit at ease and introduced himself as Sergeant Waight, our superintendent Sergeant. He then walked round the hut, stopping at every bed for a few words with each boy. When he asked me what part of Wales I came from, he raised his eyebrows in a quizzical arch when I answered 'Leeds, Sergeant,' before he continued on to the next bed. I think that was the first of many moments which I would have during the next year, when I would become more determined to seek a transfer to an 'English regiment', but there were to be many obstacles to overcome along the way.

When the two Sergeants left the hut, the TS introduced us to the first required practice which had to be rigidly adhered to: 'falling in and out!' Whenever one of us wanted to leave the room (for whatever reason), he had to go to the doorway and, after slamming both feet together, stand at the position of attention, and bellow out at the top of his voice – 'Leave to fall out, Trained Soldier please?' The TS would then answer, 'Yes, please.' A similar procedure followed when re-entering the room. This practice applied to all places and occasions, whether they be inside a barrack-room, office, or outside on the drill ground. It became second nature eventually, and it was deemed to be normal behaviour in the Guards, when joining or leaving anywhere.

On Tuesday morning at the stipulated time of five minutes before the actual time of getting on parade, Sergeant Smith's squad assembled for the very first introduction to weeks of foot drill on the small Roberts Block square, only interspersed by frantic moments as we hurriedly changed into PT kit. This consisted of blue cotton shorts (not very short in my case) and white PT vest. We would wear our brown canvas lace-up PT shoes and carry rolled-up towels. The PT shoes were known as 'Daps' in the Welsh Guards. We would then be double-marched up to the old Barracks gym and handed over to the tender care of huge men in tight navy blue trousers and blue-red-blue striped jerseys. These amateur Charles Atlases were the depot PT staff - all of them from one of the five regiments, but acting under the direction of a 'Staff Sergeant Major Instructor' from the Army Physical Training Corps. We endured one hour of PT, then we were doubled back for foot drill, and so on -throughout the long days of our training. PT included all the usual things like vaulting horses, medicine balls, climbing ropes, wall bars, etc. But just now and again, a large coir-fibre mat would be placed in the centre of the gym floor and the squad had to crowd on to it. When the PTI blew his whistle, we all had to engage in the most bruising encounter devised by some fiend at Aldershot, known as a 'melee' (but referred to by Guardsmen as 'milling'). The aim of the exercise was to attempt to be the last person left standing on the mat when the whistle blew again, and the gasping 'halt and lame' amongst our numbers would gaze with mild hatred at the bruiser left standing with puffed out chest in the mat centre! The bully-boy of our squad of course!

We were confined to barracks for the first six weeks of our depot days. Each day followed the same pattern, namely – drill, PT, shining parade each evening, more PT, drill again, a bit more drill, and then even more drill! Just in case we expected a well-earned period of inactivity at the weekends, we were to be sorely disappointed, for this was the time considered best to parade at the MI room for our 'jabs,' which were oddly referred to as 'seventy-five' or 'twenty-five' (depending on the strength of the dose, I presume). They were cruel inconveniences which resulted in painfully swollen upper arms, making the most humdrum tasks awkward to perform over the weekend.

One Saturday in particular stands out in my memory, for this was when we all were vaccinated with small-pox vaccine (most children of the twenties and thirties had been given none of these vaccinations). For our vaccination, we all queued up one behind the other and filed past two men, a medical orderly and the depot MO. With our hands on our hips we presented our bare upper arm first to the orderly who, horror of horrors, made an incision with a scalpel in our innocent flesh which he then wiped with iodine. Those of us who hadn't fainted (and there were a few!) moved on to the MO who blew a bubble of vaccine on to the cut with a glass tube which he then used to poke the vaccine well into the cut. (I shudder to think of that old-fashioned method, which was considered the norm in those days.) Many of us developed a reaction to the vaccination in varying degrees of seriousness. For my part, I managed to find myself in the depot hospital, for a period of about four days, with a violent reaction which the nursing staff called 'vaccine fever'. In most cases, a large black scab formed at the site of the vaccination, and this was protected with as strip of plaster. One had to very carefully guard against the scab being knocked off prematurely, as all sorts of complications could be the result. One poor wretch found himself in Queen Alexandra's Military Hospital, facing what passed in those days for plastic surgery, because his scab had been knocked off leaving a deep hole in his arm which showed no signs of healing. He was away for quite a while, I believe. As for the rest of us, when the scab eventually dropped off, the resultant scar was what everyone referred to as a 'vaccination mark'. On odd occasions when I catch sight of mine in a mirror these days, I think of what that little white mark cost in terms of old-fashioned medical procedures and a fair amount of discomfort!

When it came to pay day, we had to parade outside the company office hut on Thursdays to receive our pay. Drawn up in three ranks and standing easy, we would listen intently for our name being called out. At which we would answer 'Sir!' and then march in smartly, halting at attention in front of a blanket-covered trestle table, behind which would be sat my 'baby-faced' Scots Guards officer of recent memory. He, along with the Company Quartermaster Sergeant (CQMS) would receive my salute. Our weekly pay was five shillings (25p) in the hand, and about three shilings in credits. Aside from our money, every fortnight a coupon was issued to use when purchasing soap at the NAAFI. I seem to remember vaguely that we were issued with sweet coupons also, but I could rarely afford such luxuries as chocolate. Of course, we were forbidden from smoking until we reached the manly age of seventeen years, and had possession of a smoking pass!

As the weeks passed by, the pace on the drill ground intensified as Sergeant Smith prepared us for the Adjutant's sixth week inspection. Depending on our success or otherwise, the results would influence whether we would be allowed a 'walking-out pass' at last.

The day of our dreaded inspection came round at last. After the midday meal, Sergeant Smith was fussing over us one minute like a mother hen, then snapping at us like an old sheepdog the next, he was determined that he was not about to suffer his first sixth-week failure. We duly formed up for inspection and waited for the arrival of the inspecting officer. On the first stroke of 14.00 hours – accompanied by the clinking of spurs, medals, and the metallic clicks of the RSM's boots, the worthies arrived. They were greeted by our instructor, who, after bringing the squad to attention called out, 'Sergeant Smith's Boys' squad, six weeks squadded, ready for your inspection, Sir!'

The Adjutant, who was resplendent in riding breeches, highly polished boots and Sam Browne belt was a Coldstream Guards officer named Captain Darrell, (whom I was to meet in later years when he was a Brigadier). He was accompanied by the RSM of the Guards Depot, Regimental Sergeant Major Hamilton, of the Scots Guards.

After inspecting the squad by walking up and down our ranks as we stood in open order, the Adjutant gave Sergeant Smith the command to 'Carry on Sergeant please'. At which we promptly went through all our drill movements, including quick and slow marching, forming, and saluting on the march, etc. On conclusion of the squad's demonstration of foot drill movements, each individual then had to march up to the Adjutant, standing at attention three paces from him, and salute. After calling out his number, rank, name, and regiment, he would wait for the command to 'carry on' by the Adjutant. Then, after saluting again, he would turn about and rejoin the squad.

We must have come up to the prerequisite standards required by the Household Brigade and the Adjutant, because Sergeant Smith took great delight in congratulating us afterwards, and telling us not to let our standards slip from what we had achieved so far. We were now to be given a 'walking- out' pass, which would allow us to leave the confines of 'The Guards' Depot' on the following Saturday afternoon from 'after duties'. These included coal-drawing duties at 13.30 hours, so we would have to get a move on afterwards to get dressed and take advantage of our new privileges, which ended at 20.00.hours. (Yes, we all had to report back by 8 p.m.!) Meanwhile, it was a case of – 'Mothers of Croydon, lock up your daughters, the lads of Dusty Smith's squad are coming to town!'

When Saturday afternoon arrived, there was an air of excited expectancy in the hut as we all got dressed in our 'best' BD, boots, anklets, and our flipping great cheese-cutter caps! Oh, to get to the training battalion where our peaks would be cut to a respectable guardsman's pattern! We referred to the peaks on those SD caps as 'LP's' because we all felt as if we had the major part of a long-playing record stuck out over our face. In those days of gramophones and vinyl records, there were the small 'forty-five' type records, which could be found in juke boxes; then the everyday 'seventy-eight' record, which held one number on each side; and a bigger one known as an LP because it played for longer, and held more (equivalate to today's albums).

When we had subjected each other to a minute inspection, we split up into twos and threes. (No recruit would be tolerated at the barracks gate if he approached on his own). Then, 'girding our loins,' we set off bravely for the beginning of the long road leading up past the main parade ground, where we quickened our pace, swinging our arms, keeping our wits about us just in case (God forbid!) we should, by chance, encounter an officer and have to salute him, We would then salute, shouting out at the same time, 'One, two, three, four, five, down, swing!' We never stopped shouting out the accompaniment with every movement we made on the square – until we reached the week of our passing out parade.

As we marched smartly up towards the guardroom at the top of the driveway, we could see the figure of the Sergeant of the guard waiting for us. *'Please God'* I thought to myself, for it was common practice for the Sergeant to find some minor point wrong in Recruits' turn out and send them all doubling back to adjust ourselves in preparation for yet another attempt!

'Up!' called out our predetermined 'spokesman', and three pairs of boots 'crashed' crashed to a halt in front of the Sergeant. We all, in turn, shouted out our number, rank, name, and squad instructor's name as we were inspected by the Coldstream Guards Sergeant. (I never forgot his description or regiment, and can envisage him now. It's like never forgetting the registration number of your first car!) With a curt 'Off you go, lads. Don't be late back - 19.59 hours sharp!' we were allowed out of the gates for the first time in six weeks. We made our way eagerly over to the bus stop, there to wait impatiently for that chugging bus which would take us down to the delights of Croydon! (This was the limit of the permitted area within which we had to stay while out of the Barracks).

I will always remember that trip down to Croydon and the magical-sounding name of the main road - 'the Purley Way.' When we got off the bus, we noticed a big cinema frontage on the opposite side of the road. Our meagre funds would not have allowed us entry, even had we the time to indulge in such luxuries as film shows. I found out later that the cinema was the 'Davis Theatre'. One of the biggest cinemas in the country at that time, it seated hundreds and boasted a café balcony.

I wanted to get a photograph done for my parents, so they could see their 'soldier son' in uniform, so I went into a large department store called 'Kennard's Stores' where there was a photographer's studio. I had been saving up for this occasion, the session costing me the fairly large amount of 3/ 6d. I posed as suggested by the photographer, but resisted all his attempts to get me to remove my cap as I had decided no one was going to see my shaven head just yet! The photo's would be ready to pick up a couple of hours later, which time restricted my further wanderings. However, I still managed to visit the army canteen down a side street with the other lads, before paying our respects at the Saturday afternoon 'hop' being held in the East Surrey Regiment's Drill Hall – though. Dancing was out of the question for us, as we were not allowed anywhere near the dance floor with our heavy, studded ammo boots on, of course! –However, we were grateful for the teas and wads handed to us for gratis. (Probably because we had mentioned we were all on Boys' service?) Time flew quickly by as we only had a total of six hours freedom after all and very soon our wanderings had to come to an end. A couple of our number had made 'arrangements' for the following week, but that date was doomed to failure, as we were all destined to be confined to barracks, after a double innoculation session, again! A few of us had picked up photographs from Kennards, and we all agreed that they were 'good value for money'. I put all three of mine in an envelope back in the barrack hut, and decided that they would be sent to my Grandma and Mum at the next opportunity to write a letter home.

Arriving back at the depot, we sorted ourselves out into pairs, and marched smartly back through the gate and slammed our tabs in, as we approached the barrack-guard Sergeant sitting behind his desk in the guard room, pen poised for action. There were no complaints, and we all went marching back down the drive to our barrack-hut, encased in the warm glow from the Sergeant, who had complimented us all on arriving back in barracks with twenty minutes to spare. It was a little like arriving back home when we entered the barrack-hut, to be greeted by our TS with 'Fold your best BD up carefully, lads, and give your boots a clean-up. Don't forget you have got church parade tomorrow morning!'

That night I mused in bed after 'Lights Out' reliving that first taste of freedom, and relishing the thoughts about the pleasure the photographs would give back home (I hoped). I started thinking about some of the characters who had made the most impression on me during my first few weeks of army life (apart from the TS and Sergeant Smith) and wondered how many of them would figure in my future?

First and foremost was Wally Walker, a friend of mine from our schooldays in Leeds, who had been just as keen to don army uniform. He was in the Coldstream Guards, but not for long. In just a short while, his mother would secure his discharge on the grounds of him 'forging' her signature of consent for his enlistment! When he left, he made remarks in the vein of 'See you soon, Butch' (my schooldays nickname). He eventually persuaded his parents to agree to his re-enlistment, this time in The Welsh Guards – to be with me, I suppose. But by that time, my ambitions were firmly fixed on escaping from that 'foreign' regiment to join the Grenadier Guards. In 1958 Wally and I were both fellow Drum Majors on the Queen's Birthday Parade – he in the Welsh Guards and myself Grenadier Guards. When we told the story of our change round to Micky Stone (the Garrison Sergeant Major) during a brief break for tea during our Drum Majors' refresher training week with him, he thought the twist of fate was a hoot!

Another character that made an impression on me in our squad was a boy called Peter Billyield, who had come all the way from British Guyana to enlist in the Irish Guards of all things! His unusual accent marked him out for special attention from the emerging bully boys in the squad, and I remember one occasion when they strung him up to the roof trussing of the hut, leaving him there to miss a dinner meal. They thought it a huge jape, and warned off anyone who tried to free him! Tough times were to continue for the poor little chap, and they made his life hell before he finally escaped their clutches at the conclusion of our depot training, and departed for Lingfield racecourse and the Irish Guards Training Battalion there. (I wonder what happened to him?) The demand created by the recent hostilities of World War 2 for extra army accommodation had caused some strange requisitions of buildings and land. As a result, the Welsh Guards Training Battalion was also based on a racecourse at Sandown Park in Esher, Surrey.

The bullies, who 'hunted in a pack' were about three or four boys from the mining areas of South Wales. They seemed determined to stamp their mantle of control over all in the squad, and that 'knock about' existence sucked me in also for the next year, making my life intolerable until I took up boxing!

I must have dozed off with Billyield on my mind because I had a fitful night's sleep that night, or could it have been the excitement generated by our visit to Croydon? On Sunday morning after breakfast we paraded outside the hut, along with the other three Boys' squads, and were duly marched up to the depot chapel for the obligatory church parade. A couple of lads had gone elsewhere in the barracks because they were 'arsees' (RC's) as some Welsh wag told us. Of course, they were actually Roman Catholic boys who went to their own church down in the 'Fox' lines somewhere for Sunday Mass.

I had always been encouraged by my parents in my religious upbringing and at the outbreak of War, as very young soprano, had just passed my audition to become a probationer in the choir of Leeds Parish Church under the wing of the notorious Dr Melville Cook, a well-known church-Organist and Master-of- choristers in those days. Eventually the outbreak of WWII and my subsequent evacuation 'to a place of safety' knocked that on the head for me, but I joined a little parish church choir instead in Otley, the town where I was evacuated.

As I sat in the depot chapel that day, looking along the rows of shaven heads sported by the hundreds of Recruits sat in their regimental groups, I started to feel part of an elite brotherhood, which the stirring music from the regimental band of the Coldstream Guards contributed too in no small measure!

Apart from the satisfaction I derived from those church parades in a comradely way, I also felt the fresh awakenings of a dormant religious calling. This was to stay with me for the rest of my life, a life which promised to be, and became fruitful in many ways, with so many exciting moments along its long diverse path!

As the tempo increased towards that seemingly unachievable objective – our 'pass out' – we became almost over confident about our daily training routine, allowed ourselves the odd boyish joke and giggle (boys will be boys!) as we drifted out of the hut each morning for the first drill period of the day. We generally seemed to have the little square at the side of Roberts Block to ourselves most mornings for that first hour, before doubling off to our PT training in the gym as the next squad took our place for their foot drill training. The Superintendant Sergeant, Sergeant Waight, Scots Guards, presumably had a chart in his bunk on which all his squads were moved about from place to place as he juggled the intricacies of planning the 'quart-in-a-pint-pot' programme of training which our restricted facilities placed on him each day.

Sergeant Waight was a typical example of a Guards Sergeant in those times, just after the war, his tough craggy exterior and seemingly harsh manner hiding a much gentler nature. When he wanted to speak to a squad, he never interrupted the instructor (in our case, Sergeant Smith) but waited for an appropriate moment to present itself. I only heard his voice rise in anger once away from the drill ground, and it was for a very good reason.

Our ever-present Superintending Sergeant 'lived in' – in other words, he did not have his family with him at the depot in married quarters, preferring that his children continued with their schooling back home in Scotland. However, it was common knowledge that he was picking up his chocolate ration each week, and saving it in his bunk towards Christmas when, after all of his squads would have departed to their training battalions, he could take some well-earned leave back home with his own young ones. Some stupid characters decided to help themselves to a share of the little Christmas hoard of chocolate one night, when the Sergeant was away from his 'bunk' (single room) relaxing in the Sergeants' mess.

All hell erupted the next morning when we were bundled out of our huts at reveille to stand shivering and blinking, while an extremely irate Scots Guards Sergeant stomped up and down in front of the assembled boys. He let us know, first of all, about his low opinion of the boy or boys who had committed this heinous crime. Secondly he said that this bad behaviour had tainted his opinion of every boy present! (Additional shivers ran through the assembled ranks at this observation.) His crimson face gradually assumed its more normal sallow appearance as he exhausted his vocabulary, and he started to become more like the Sergeant Waight we all knew and respected. He closed his reprimands, by promising an end to the matter if the said chocolates were returned untouched as soon as he dismissed us. At breakfast, there was a heated discussion and dire promises of the resultant action when (and if) we found out for ourselves who the perpetrators were. We were all quite young, the oldest ones only barely sixteen years of age, and it was natural therefore for us to regard the Sergeant as a 'father figure' and had any of us known who the culprits were, I don't think they would have been unbruised when we finally 'shopped' them! Needless to say, therefore, that when the Sergeant returned from breakfast he found the chocolate returned and intact on his bed, so no more was said about the incident, but it left a nasty taste in our mouths for a few days, and the petty thief (or thieves) remained undiscovered.

There was another more serious case of a disciplinary nature when some Irish Guards boys made a complaint, to the Adjutant of the Irish Guards Training Battalion at Lingfield, about the bad treatment they had experienced at the hands of their squad instructor at the Guards Depot. An investigation took place, which resulted in the entire squad members being brought back to the Guards Depot from their respective training battalions to give evidence during the hearing of the complaint against Lance-Sergeant 'A' - their depot squad instructor. It had not escaped our notice that this particular instructor had re-appeared in our midst, but only in as much as he was confined to an NCO's (Non Comissioned Officer) bunk in Roberts Block, with a Guardsman stood outside the door. It wouldn't have been good form, I suppose, for him to be placed in the depot guard-room. We were quite envious of the Boys from the training battalions, as they all were sporting 'cut' peaks, and had a light-green blanco on their web belts and anklets. In these days, with the differing attitudes of NCOs in the Guards, the basis of the Boys' complaints would appear to be frivolous. But in those times of the forties however, they were very serious indeed as the Lance-Sergeant was accused of abusing the boys in his squad by the use of offensive and obscene language in his dealings with them! I believe he was 'reprimanded', and warned about his future behaviour when supervising Recruits, specifically enlisted Boys. I can't imagine the matter having any major repercussions for him though, as I remember him as a Sergeant in the Regiment later on after my transfer to the Grenadier Guards. The boys concerned in the case went back to their training battalions, and nothing further was heard of the case.

Talking of present-day attitudes and behaviour brings me to the accepted practice of 'nude beaches' and the tolerance shown to nudism generally. However, it was a shock, to us products of the late twenties and thirties, when we were introduced to 'skinny dipping' at the Guards Depot swimming bath! We had no swimming trunks to wear though, even if they had they been allowed. We had been getting used to the sight of each other's naked form ever since the first week, as a result of having to adopt the practice of going 'two in each shower' after PT, but the sight of every member of the squad stood on the pool side, naked as the day we were born was a new revelation (in more ways than one!).

Swimming formed a necessary part of our physical training and took place in a large single-storey building with a few small windows in the upper part of the walls. A huge iron stove stood in each corner of the hall to provide heating (there was no central heating in those days), and in the centre was the large swimming pool, encircled by a concrete edge. We just dropped our PT shorts where we stood and were formed up at the shallow end trying to appear nonchalant, but conscious nevertheless, about our small underdeveloped physiques, the legacy of war time rationing! I had no qualms about this makeshift introduction to swimming instruction, as I had learned to swim at my grammar school, but other less fortunate souls were soon floundering about like trainee seals! The water temperature was absolutely perishing and conducive towards rapid movement once you had been in for a few seconds. I think I passed the basic requirements as no comments came my way from the PTIs, but others were less fortunate, being subjected to a watery hellish experience each time we entered that dreaded place!

Our physical training attainments (or otherwise) were subject to examination in the form of a series of practical tests over a week towards the end of our time at the Guards Depot. On the first day we had to perform all sorts of gymnastic exercises involving the vaulting horses, wall bars, ceiling ropes and medicine balls with verbal encouragement and under the supervision of two PTIs while an Army Physical Training Corps Staff Sergeant stood making notes on sheets of paper attached to a mill board. The next day we were taken to the small running track, at the rear of Roberts Block, where we had to run varying timed distances around the cinder track, all of which culminated in the most demanding of all – the 100-yards sprint!

Heaven knows what would have happened had we been found wanting in our physical prowess at these exams – would we have been 'back-squadded,' I wonder?

That 'hellish' gym was also the place of lighter moments when we had the dubious pleasure of the ENSA shows, which we all were required to attend. These were on Saturday evenings, so they weren't exactly popular with anyone. As usual with the British Tommy during the war, those wonderful folks in ENSA had, despite the excellent entertainment they provided in all theatres of war and at home, attracted the 'tongue-in-cheek' description of 'Every Night Something Awful'. Speaking for myself, I thought they provided quite a good show on those occasions when I sat through the performances at the Guards Depot. There were always some nice legs on show from the dancing girls too! Consorting with members of the opposite sex was absolutely forbidden for enlisted boys, but I did strike up a conversation with a pretty girl one Saturday afternoon at the forces canteen in Croydon, which resulted in an invitation to her home for a 'cup of tea' with her parents. I didn't appreciate the howls of laughter and ribald comments from her father on first exposing my shorn head when I removed my cap, but he proved to be quite hospitable over tea. He had been in a 'reserved occupation' during the war, so I was spared from any worldly advice from an old soldier. I had experienced that from my dad when I left home some time ago.

I had to leave after a short while to catch my bus back up to Caterham, but on the way to my bus stop, the girl suggested that we go off the path and in to some bombed-out shop premises nearby for a 'kiss and cuddle' (her words). No sooner had we gotten out of sight, than she pushed me up gainst a wall, plonked her lips on mine, and started fumbling with my flies, for heavens' sake! It took me about three seconds to scramble out of her clutches and scamper along the pavement to the main road, where I was just in time to jump thankfully on to the platform of the bus back to the Guards Depot and relative 'safety'. Given a few years, it may have ended quite differently of course! A lesson well learned for the future, and it was quite evident that she was keeping well out of my way when I visited the forces canteen again (with three companions this time, thank goodness!).

I had reconciled myself early on in my recruits' course to the fact that there was little chance of me joining the ranks of a Guard's regimental band, despite the bland assurances to the contrary from the Recruiting Warrant Officer in Leeds. (Although fate had decreed that I would march in front of all the Guards regimental bands in the future).

One afternoon each week was given over to instruction on side-drum, bugle and flute by Sergeant Bridges of the Scots Guards, who was in charge of the Guards Depot Corps of Drums. This was a small but very proficient group numbering about a dozen side-drummers and flautists, who were also skilled buglers who did their stint as duty bugler on guard, when required. A few boys in the Irish and Scots Guards expressed a desire to learn to play the bagpipes, and they were given 'chanter' lessons by one of the two Scots Guards pipers on the depot staff, one of whom was a Lance Corporal. These two stalwarts manned the depot post bunk, and were responsible for handling all the depot mail, both 'in' and 'out.' They were dressed all the time in khaki Service-Dress jackets (with brass buttons), and Royal Stuart tartan trews, all topped off with their glengarry headgear.

When a Scots Guards recruit squad had passed out, and was ready to leave for the Scots Guards Training Battalion at Pirbright, one of the pipers would play them down to Caterham Railway Station. The Guardsmen (as they were now), responded well to this gesture, and would strut along with that extra pride of their regiment, on their way to join more experienced comrades.

We knew that we were getting closer to our departure when Sergeant Smith started preparing us for our final 'passing out' parade, after which we would leave the depot on conclusion of our basic recruits' course. The Boys' training period was of slightly less duration than the adult recruits', due to us not having arms drill in our curriculum. As enlisted Boys we were not allowed to 'bear arms' of course.

When the great day of our 'pass out' dawned, TS Smith fussed around us like a mother hen all morning, as we put that extra coat of gloss on boots and cap straps, or conjured up yet a more brilliant sparkle (if that were possible!) from belt brasses and cap badges. The afternoon session with the Adjutant loomed ever nearer! When we 'walked' very carefully on to the edge of the drill ground, ready to receive the final 'Get on . . . parade!' from Sergeant Smith, I think we were all feeling that little touch of 'stage fright'. That soon passed, however, once our Instructor had spent a couple of minutes calming us all down, by telling us all just to concentrate on his words of command, and to think before answering if asked a question by the Adjutant – Captain Darrell MC. Needless to say, thanks to all those weeks of dedicated excellence from Sergeat Smith, we all passed with flying colours and, though still on parade, could not fail but to heave a collective sigh of relief as the jingling of the Adjutant's spurs and medals faded away in the distance. We had finished with all those hours of concentrated foot drill at last! The next day, while our 'passing out' dress was still at its best, we had our squad photograph taken. I thought my chest would burst with pride when Sergeant Smith said, 'I want two smart lads to stand in the two flank spaces at the ends of the middle row – and they will be Boy Rice, and you - Boy Angell'.

That squad photograph is so precious to me, (I could only afford to buy one copy). Over the years, for one reason or another, it became quite damaged; however, it is still possible to detect the pride in the stance of 'Pudding' Rice and myself!

The following morning the Scots Guards and Coldstream Guards Boys departed for Pirbright Camp and their respective training battalions, followed the next day by the Grenadier Guards to Windsor, and the Irish Guards lads to Lingfield. I couldn't help smiling at the evident glee on Peter Billyield's face as he shook himself free from his Welsh Guards tormentors! – (I never heard of him again).

I remember to this day that final night in our echoing hut, empty except for the beds of the TS and the Welsh Guards Boys. We gathered round the stove as dear old Dusty Smith regaled us with stories about his exploits in the recent war, and his travels in the Middle East with the Fifth Battalion Grenadier Guards. He would not be drawn on the details of the wounds we knew he had picked up somewhere along the way. We were going to miss him, and I think he would miss most of us for a while, although I suspect he had certain misgivings about one or two of the Welsh Guards boys. He was going on privilege leave after our departure, then it seemed he was going to rejoin the 'Fourteenth Company' Grenadier Guards in the main barracks - as a mens' Recruits' squad Trained Soldier once more.

Sergeant Smith took the opportunity to see old friends in the Welsh Guards, by accompanying us to the training battalion at Sandown Park racecourse in Esher. The march down to Caterham Railway Station in full 'change of quarters order' proved testing by putting quite a weight on our skinny frames! – as did the distance from Esher station up to Sandown Park race course, the home of the training battalion of The Welsh Guards, with its long entry drive testing us further! As we reached the top of the drive alongside the parade ground (car park in more peaceful times), we were met by the diminutive figure of little Drum Major 'Mush' Williams. He was only five feet, eight inches tall, and was dwarfed by the height of Sergeant Smith.

After a few words with the Drum Major, our squad instructor left us, with a friendly 'goodbye lads, be good!' as we were now the responsibility of someone else. Sergeant Smith had proved to be a wonderful introduction to what a Sergeant had to endure when he was presented with a bunch of raw recruits, and being required to mould them in to young Guardsmen, or Boys in our case. From our very first few days at the demanding Guards Depot, he had treated us all in a fair but firm manner. He never referred once to my English origins. I think he recognised that some of the Welsh Boys were forming a clique, and stamped that out immediately. I knew, however, that they would reform their little gang just as soon as we were away from his eagle eye! He was another nice chap from my early army days who I never saw again which was a pity!

With a curt 'follow me, boys,' the Drum Major took us to a small block which stood on its own at the top of the drive, in better times it was the 'press box.' Inside the single-storey building, we entered a room which contained about twelve two-tier bunk beds, complete with 'biscuit' three-piece matresses on each bed.

'This is where you will be billeted when you come back from leave,' said the Drum Major, 'and this Is Corporal Evans who will be in charge of you then.' 'Brilliant!' I thought. We were to go home almost immediately after our tea meal. A small man (I was going to have to adapt to these smaller figures of authority in the Corps of Drums) stepped forward. He was a Welshman obviously and spoke with a definite South Wales accent. Within the first half hour, it became obvious also that he wasn't particularly keen on Englishmen in his national regiment. *'Oh god-not another one!'* I thought ruefully.

Matters proceeded at whirlwind speed after that first meeting with the Drum Major and our Corporal, as we were whisked through packing up our kit and handing it in at the drum stores, which was situated in one of the grandstands. We were then marched to our tea meal in the mess room (previously the race goers' restaurant), which is where we were told we would be required to sit for all our meals in future. The huge mess hall was empty, except for some ATS girls from the orderly room who were having an early meal. I noticed that they all sported the glittering Welsh Guards leek badge above the left breast pocket of their khaki service-dress jackets. Each one's hair was coiled neatly round the head with the obligatory blonde quiff at the front just like Mum's. Mum would cut the top off stocking legs and, after pulling the hoop round her head, she would then coil her hair round it until she had a roll of hair going round her head just above the ears. Besides being very attractive, that style was a good added safety feature under her turban at her war work.

As the Regiments settled down to a peace time existence once more, all the ATS girls were withdrawn gradually from the army units in which they had been acting as clerks or officers' servants, etc. (at home stations in Blighty). They seemed to vanish almost overnight from the Guards regiments sometime in the early part of 1946. They all smiled at us, but there was no attempt at conversation. I suppose they had been 'warned off' us young 'innocents'!

At one point, the Corporal called out 'Boys – shun!' but there came an immediate reply of 'Carry on please, Corporal Evans' from the tall majestic figure walking across the room to where we were eating. 'I just wanted to make sure that all the Boys had arrived, and were being settled in.' The owner of the deep melodious voice, which had just a faint Welsh lilt, was immaculately dressed in khaki service-dress and gleaming Sam Browne belt. On his sleeves were the huge 'Royal Arms' of a Guards' Regimental Sergeant Major. He wore a black Welsh Guards forage cap with gold braid on the peak. This was our first contact with Sergeant Major 'Mickey' Dunne, a great character with an impressive word of command also. Like Sergeant Smith before him, he proved to be one of the more pleasant men in the Welsh Guards. After a few words with each one of our little group, he left us to finish our meal. After we finished eating, we queued up outside the Drum Major's office, which was in one of a row of stables running down an alleyway. After receiving our leave passes and rail warrants from Esher to our home stations, we received a few words of advice from him about dress and behaviour on leave, and were dismissed to proceed on our homeward journeys.

We were a small excited group as we walked all the way to the railway station where we were to catch the train from Esher to Waterloo, where we split up with cries of 'Merry Christmas! See ya!' and made our separate ways to the various mainline stations to catch the various trains home. On arriving at King's Cross, after an impatient ride on the tube, I found I had to wait until 23.20 hours (I was getting used to this twenty-four-hour clock already) when I would be able to catch a 'troop train.' We still had these trains which were reserved for the sole use of the forces to relieve the pressure on civilian requirements. The post-war release programme had not gotten fully into its stride at this time, it was only four months since VJ Day after all, so there was a huge demand on the railways to provide transport for the armed forces. By the time my train departed from King's Cross, it was packed in every space available with sailors, soldiers, and quite a few lads and lasses in Air Force blue, all bound homewards for their very first peace time break from duties.

I had to content myself with a standing space in the corridor for quite a long time, until the first people got off, and I was lucky enough to find a seat in a compartment, and promptly got my head down for some much-needed sleep. The journey home was hell! I think the railway authorities must have chosen all the 'back lines' for the use of troop trains, and we made our way north with many stops for no apparent reason. I didn't arrive in Leeds Central station until about 08.45 the next morning. I wonder how the travelling public these days would relish a journey taking approximately ten hours just to get from London to Leeds?

It was very pleasant to ride home from Leeds city centre to the suburbs on a tramcar, which now had a nice open view through windows having been stripped of their war time anti shatter gauze netting. As I strode up the hill after alighting from the tram, I noticed a man coming out of a shop opening a packet of twenty Senior Service cigarettes. Gone were the 'No cigarettes, sorry, only Abdullas' (Turkish) outside that shop. There were evidently going to be quite a few changes for me to discover now things had improved in the few months since the end of the war.

I finally reached home and as if by some prearranged signal, the door flew open at the top of our 'area' steps, and there stood my mum - beaming all over her face. My youngest brother Reggie was jumping up and down with excitement at her side as a black whirlwind suddenly pushed through their legs and bounded down the steps to throw himself on me with woofs and licks! I had been away from home for less than three months, but that must have seemed like three years to 'Chum', my lovely Labrador dog, who had shared many nights curled up with me in our cellar during the latter years of the war time air raids. After receiving his share of pats and cuddles, he proceeded to lead the way for me up the steps to where my mum stood with open arms. As my mum enfolded me in a huge cuddle, all the last three months faded away. I was back home in the bosom of my family again, even if that time was restricted by the army to a mere ten days for Christmas! My dad stood just behind mum, patiently waiting to greet his soldier son with a bear hug. Then, with a grin at my 'cheese-cutter' SD cap, he quipped 'If you can't fight – wear a big hat!'. He knew I was proud of his war time service, and I hoped that I could make him just as proud of me in the future.

CHAPTER 13

A BOY SOLDIER OF THE KING- PART 2

MY PRECIOUS TEN DAYS Christmas leave at home came to an end far too quickly, and I soon found myself on an equally slow train heading back to Surrey, via London, and life in a new army station where I would only meet Welsh Guards personnel. On our return from liberty, we started to adapt to life in a battalion, but some of the rules which someone had decided were the 'norm' for young lads, were more draconian than anything we had experienced at the Guards Depot.

Reveille was at 06.30 every morning, Sundays included, and through the door would crash our Corporal (the one who didn't care for English lads, me in particular!) with a loud shout of 'Up you come, lively now, and get those smelly little hands and faces washed. And don't forget, you all have to shave now!' This he said with daily variations, but he never, ever, forgot to slap his hand on my pillow – why mine?

At 07.00 we formed up outside our billet in denim jackets and trousers, carrying our mugs and 'eating irons' while the Corporal inspected us from the tops of our heads to the tips of our highly polished boots. We were all starting to get our hair a little more civilised since those first weeks of sporting bald heads at the 'Guards Depot,' but that didn't stop this disciplinarian from telling at least one of us to 'get your bloody hair cut!' every day, and I was picked out to be told this on the very first day, of course! We then were marched by him down a narrow cobbled alleyway with stable doors on one side (minus racehorses for now until the training battalion moved and that was to come much sooner than any of us knew at the time) until we entered the mess room where we found the meals to be slightly better than the excellent scoff we had enjoyed at the depot. As my time in Sandown progressed, I must confess that there were the odd moments when I felt I was back at the depot . . . Strange!

After a hard day of drills, music lessons, instrument tuition and practice we had to stand on our beds barefooted, wearing just our khaki shirts and underpants with our hands held out so that our Corporal (sometimes the Drum Major himself) could inspect our hands and feet for cleanliness. Every Sunday evening, we had to give a letter home for our parents to the Corporal with the flap unsealed. I tried to tell my mum and dad about the way the Corporal was singling me out (or so it seemed to me in those early days), but I wasn't very adept at that young age for putting thoughts into words, so I'm afraid they were left thinking that although my life was a bit harsh, like my days at naval school, I was settling down at last. (Oh no, I wasn't!)

The Drum Major was a very small man for the Guards. If a Drummer Boy didn't reach the height that the Guards expected by the time he was eighteen and a Drummer, then it was tough luck for the regiment as it had to honour his enlistment. Our Drum Major had been a Drummer Boy before the war, he had a bald patch in the dark hair on the back of his head, the legacy of a German hand-grenade splinter which sliced some of his scalp.

I found him to be more pleasant than the Corporal, and I could have kissed him (well, perhaps not!) when he gave me the job of tenor drummer in the playing Corps of Drums on a couple of Sundays when we marched the battalion past the 'Winning Post' milk bar, on the way to church. (I had made the acquaintance of a very nice girl on a visit to the 'Winning Post' one time. She worked in the café at Chessington Zoo and had treated me to a cuppa and a bun there too!) The Battalion attended church every week, but due to the small capacity of the building, only a couple of companies could attend each week in turn.

One week I was feeling really groggy and had to attend sick parade, which entailed us wearing full battle dress, but we were excused from wearing our web anklets on this occasion. We did however have to carry our small pack containing a pair of clean socks, a change of linen and our toilet bits and pieces. When it was my turn to see the MO, he sounded my chest with his stethoscope and tapped all over my back with his hand, then after a few words from him to the medical Sergeant, I found myself in the back of a fifteen-hundred-weight truck on my way to hospital, where I was to stay for over five weeks suffering from what? They didn't seem to know, and I had all sorts of tests in the hospital. One involved a long ride in an ambulance to a hospital called 'Botley Park' in another part of Surrey for deep X-rays, etc.

The hospital I was to stay in for my period of 'getting better' (the matron's words) was called the 'Schiff Home of Recovery', and it was situated in a large area of parkland in the village of Cobham. It was a civilian hospital, but there was a ward given over for the treatment of military patients. All the nurses took pity on this strange little lad in army uniform, but I became the target of some very special care from a very pretty young Irish nurse, who was exceptionally kind to me. When I was allowed out of bed eventually she would accompany me for short walks along the corridors, after fussily ensuring that I was properly 'wrapped up' in my pyjamas and hospital dressing gown. She was an angel to this Angell! There was a central glass-roofed circular room provided for reading, and to my delight, there was also a grand piano where I would tinkle the keys occasionally when there was no other person there who might have objected to the intrusion. I was also to benefit from one of the sisters (who was always on nights for some reason) when she found out that I only got 5s. for a week's pay. She would often slip a 2s. coin on the top of my bedside locker and the occasional bag of sweets too. When Sister discovered I had been a choirboy in Civvy Street, she took me to a service one Sunday morning in the nearby parish church, slipping a sixpence in my pocket for the collection too! The folks in the congregation seemed quite puzzled to see such a young chap wearing hospital blues, the compulsory wear at that time for military personnel in hospital, but there I was in blue trousers held up by a drawcord at the waist, blue jacket, white shirt, and red tie, with only my khaki service dress cap bearing the regimental brass leek design badge to mark me out as a military patient. This outfit still meant a lot to the civilians of the forties as the wearer was generally recovering from wounds, but of course, I had no visible signs to give a clue about the nature of my obvious disability, being accompanied by a nursing sister in uniform and cape!

One day I was allowed out to visit the afternoon matinee at the local cinema, and as it was a bit further away from the hospital gates than I felt capable of tackling on foot, I waited for the bus to take me there. When I boarded the bus, the conductress took one look at the hospital blue and waved me to a seat on the lower deck, telling me to put the money back in my pocket! I got the same treatment at the cinema cash desk and, during the film show interval, I felt a slim hand on my shoulder, and a tub of ice cream was placed in my hand by a young usherette with a lovely smile as she sat at my side, chatting to me until the house lights faded for the second half of the show. I was shown such kindness that day, and I felt a bit of a fraud really, for I was only poorly. I hadn't experienced any of the military side of war (then), but I had sat nearly every night in our air raid shelter at home, existing on the low diet caused by wartime rationing for six years. We on the home front went through our own part of the war and its hardships.

The day dawned eventually when the doctors and nursing staff at the hospital had to kick me out, so on went my uniform again in exchange for my hospital blues (which I handed in a bit reluctantly, I must confess). With a farewell kiss from Sister, who had stayed in after her night shift ended to see me off, a tearful hug and a whispered

'Take care of yourself, mind now,' from my Irish nurse, I got in the jeep which was waiting for me. With a wave, I was on my way back to the battalion in Esher!

Life for me was miserable over the next few months, only improving slightly when the individual training battalions in the Brigade of Guards were disbanded to be amalgamated into two new Guards training battalions. At that point I found myself once again mixing with boys from all the other regiments in the Second Guards Training Battalion at Pirbright Camp near Woking, but still in the county of Surrey and within spitting distance of the British Army's 'ancestral home' of Aldershot! The First Guards Training battalion was at Windsor, and it was there that some of the young guardsmen got their first taste of public duties by performing Castle Guard duties for forty-eight hours at a time, confined to the castle guardroom except for their turn on sentry duty for two hours—a duty they would learn to refer to as being 'on stag.'

As time progressed at Pirbright, the experience of mixing with boys of the other Guards regiments made me very unsettled with life in the Welsh Guards, so I 'girded my loins' and made a formal application to transfer to the Grenadier Guards. When the day dawned for my application to be heard by the commandant, I had visions of moving my kit to the Grenadiers boys' barracks room that afternoon, but that was not to be. As it transpired, I would have to stay in the Welsh Guards for a few months until I reached the age of seventeen years and six months, the day when my boy's service ended and I started the six months which heralded my eighteenth birthday and the commencement of my regular term of the enlisted nine years with the Colours and three years in the Army Reserve that I had signed up for.

I will draw a curtain over the few months spent with the Welsh Guards, during which time we moved to the Guards Depot at Caterham for some reason and were billeted in the same block as the depot Corps of Drums, a very small but talented playing corps with men drawn from all five regiments. I remained there until the day dawned when I finally packed my kit, and off I went down to

Caterham Railway Station and on to Chelsea Barracks in London to join the First Battalion Grenadier Guards, which had just returned home after completing its wartime role as a motorised battalion fighting in France and Germany alongside the Guards Armoured Division.

The battalion was at its wartime establishment of four rifle companies, a support company comprised of the ant-tank, mortar, and medium machine gun platoons, and the headquarter company. Life took on a more exciting and interesting aspect for me during that year of 1947, as the battalion took on its royal duties of providing the King's Guards at Buckingham Palace, St James's Palace, the Bank of England, and the Tower of London too, but the three most memorable things that year were my first sighting of the King, when we were part of the King's Birthday Parade in June on Horse Guards Parade, and the first meetings of many with HRH Princess Elizabeth, the colonel of our regiment.

In April we were drawn up as a battalion on the parade ground at Chelsea Barracks to be reviewed by our colonel to mark her twenty first birthday and, in my case, the very first close-up of this lovely young lady. She inspected the regimental band and the Corps of Drums first, and as she passed by me, a vision in a pretty polka-dot dress, I gazed into her blue eyes for a fleeting moment as she moved away to inspect the lines of the companies. Then something happened, which I have never forgotten. It started to rain, and as if by magic, a huge umbrella opened over the head of our royal visitor. Right on cue, the band started to play 'Isn't This a Lovely Day (To Be Caught in the Rain)?' and I heard a little girlish giggle coming from the lines of the King's Company. The qualifying height at that time was six feet and over for the Guards, with many of them towering well above that lofty stature too. The Princess was about to inspect the giant guardsmen who served and she appeared tiny in comparison. What a memorable first encounter with the Royal Family and a realisation that now I really was a 'soldier of the King'.

In November of that year, I felt honoured again to be stood with the band and drums, together with the guard of honour provided by the King's Company facing the entrance of Westminster Abbey for the wedding of our beloved colonel to the dashing young naval lieutenant HRH Prince Phillip of Greece. What a memorable beginning to my life as a British grenadier!

1947 saw me transfer out of the Welsh Guards and into the Grenadiers. I had no quarrel with that great Welsh regiment per se, just with a few who had a dislike of this English lad wearing Welsh Guards designations on his shoulder and made it known to me in various ways. I could put all that behind me now, including the memory of that bullying Welsh Corporal thank goodness. These days, of course, he would be regarded as a racist having such a dislike for the English boys under his command.

CHAPTER 14
'ALL IS NOT WELL, SIR!'

I FELT SETTLED IN my new role as a drummer with the Grenadiers, and that first year of 1947 was when I felt happier with my lot than had ever been the case when serving as a boy in the Welsh Guards.

The First Battalion Grenadier Guards was stationed in Chelsea barracks when I first joined them.

The guard mounting parade was a huge affair when drawn up on the square at Chelsea, comprising of the following:

1. Saint James's Palace detachment of the King's Guard
2. Buckingham Palace detachment
3. Main Guard Tower of London
4. Spur Guard Tower of London
5. Magazine Guard
6. Prisoner of War Guard
7. Barracks Guard
8. Inlying Picquet
9. Men in Waiting

The King's Guard was for forty-eight hours, I think, at the time. And because the war had held up essential works at Buckingham Palace, the guardroom was based on the ground floor of the block nearest to the barracks guardroom at Wellington Barracks. We were dressed in khaki Battle Dress in those days, with khaki greatcoats, webbing belt, shoulder straps and anklets. The sentries carried .303 Lee Enfield rifles, and the officers wore Webley Pistols. I seem to remember that the guardsmen also carried their two webbing ammo pouches on their belts. All our web equipment was blancoed with the battalion regulation khaki/green 103.

One occasion remains fixed in my memory when I was the drummer of the Buckingham Palace detachment, where —besides cleaning the kit of the sergeant of the guard, I accompanied the patrols during the night, carrying a paraffin lantern. All reliefs had to enter the palace grounds via the police station gate in Buckingham Palace Road, because the palace guardroom and post office were in the hands of the works department while the new boiler house was installed. (A process that took quite a few weeks if I remember correctly.)

The incident, which remains as a treasured memory of one of the many hilarious moments of my wonderful life in the regiment, occurred one wintry night. I was accompanying the captain, the sergeant, and two guardsmen for a patrol of the posts in the palace grounds and those mounted on the posts on the pavement outside the palace (they were still outside at that time).

I led the way, carrying the lantern, and off we tramped out of Wellington Barracks and through the side gate to wend our way to the rear of the palace. I seem to remember that the two posts there were numbers 6 and 6a, the latter being at the far end near the swimming pool part of the palace. As we approached number 6, we were met by the sound of the sentry slamming his feet on the gravel, sloping arms in readiness for our halt. As we did, he gave smart butt salute.

'Number 6 post, Buckingham Palace Guard, and all's well, sir!', came his report.

After the captain asked him a few questions about his beat, he gave another butt salute as we started on our way towards post 6a. But instead of going back to his 'at ease' position, he suddenly called after us, 'He's not down there, sir. He's here with me!' The patrol halted, turned about, and stood there while the captain and sergeant retraced their steps to find the other sentry inside the sentry box of number 6 post.

A rapid cross examination elicited the information that the guard from 6a post 'thought he had seen a shape', and being of a very nervous disposition, had immediately beat a hasty retreat to cower inside the box of, and behind, his fellow sentry! I will leave you to draw your own conclusions of what happened eventually. Enough to say that, in the short term, one of the guardsmen in our patrol took over number 6a post, and after cutting the rest of the patrol short, we took the nervous offender under escort back to the palace guardroom in Wellington Barracks. I seem to remember he ended up in the guardroom back at Chelsea Barracks. We were told not to spread the story, but these incidents are the stuff of life to guardsmen, aren't they? And it was a topic of ribald re-enactment in the NAAFI canteen for quite some time.

I can't remember the poor chap's name, but even if I could, you may rest assured I would *not* tell. Not now — seventy-three years later!

CHAPTER 15

BROTHERS IN KHAKI

IN LATE 1947 THE battalion left London for Victoria Barracks in Windsor, and I soon learned to love that station.

I have happy memories of my early friendship with a certain Guardsman, Derek 'Les' Owlett, a member of the motor transport platoon. It was not unusual for drummers and guardsmen to socialise together and I found that this new pal of mine was one of the most likeable and un-assuming I was destined to meet during my army service.

We were thrown together as friends because of our shared dating of two inseparable girls, and we started meeting every night in a little pub in Windsor called the Star, where we would spend hours singing to the accompaniment of a jukebox. Our favourite songs were those foot-tapping dance tunes with words. On Saturday evenings we could be found tripping our way round the dance floor at the Mechanics' Institute Hall in Sheet Street, usually finishing off at the Falcon Café with pie and mushy peas—a plateful for a shilling!

Our few months in Windsor were occupied by providing the guards for Windsor Castle, the Berkshire home of the royal family and the preparations for our impending deployment overseas to Palestine on active service. All our inoculations were brought up to date during these preparations and because news had been received of a cholera epidemic in Egypt where we were to spend some time in a transit camp, we all received an anti-cholera jab. This was one of the most painful injections I can remember ever receiving and we all had very sore arms for quite a while until it's after effects gradually ceased, thank goodness. I have had hundreds of needles stuck in my body over the years for various reasons, including yellow fever and typhus too, but never one of them as unpleasant as that anti-cholera injection and its after-effects!

In early March we embarked on the Troopship *Empire Pride* for Palestine via a short stay in Egypt and further years in North Africa, not to return until September 1951. One of the memorable events during that voyage occurred when we were sailing through the Straits of Gibraltar. We were lined up on deck facing the African coast, just a few miles away to starboard, while the adjutant went into the details of the Battle of Tangier, where the regiment gained its first battle honour in 1680. He made it sound as if the action had only taken place yesterday, stressing his tale with occasional pointing with his outstretched arm, sweeping in the direction of the sandy strip of coastline. I have never forgotten that history lesson given almost at the site of the Battle of Tangier in 1680!

One night as we drew nearer to Egypt, I stood on deck enjoying the soft Mediterranean breeze when I became aware of Les, my best buddy, standing at my side.

'Cop for that big pub sign 'ower there, Rod!' he exclaimed and, following his pointing finger, I saw the biggest illuminated Johnny Walker whisky sign ever just clearing the eastern horizon. For the next couple of hours, we just stood watching the Egyptian port of Port Said growing ever larger until the sergeant major came to us.

'Right, lads, that's enough for now. Back to your hammocks. We disembark in a few hours.'

For the next couple of weeks, we were based in the Number 256 Transit Camp on the opposite bank of the Suez Canal from Port Said in Port Foudd until we could embark on a smaller troopship for our onward journey to the Port of Haifa in Palestine.

Les and I took the opportunity to explore the town of Port Said and get our first experience of 'the Mystic East'! Away from our two girls in Windsor, we became even closer to one another. I remember one night we were amazed by a 'gilly-gilly boy' who seemed determined to persuade us to go with him to witness the indelicate show of, as he put it, 'pretty little lady with donkey just for you, johnny!' and other dodgy offers. He followed us for a few yards, bearing in mind that we had been warned about these Oriental spivs, we went on our way without responding. He then said 'OK, johnny, just for you donkey with monkey, huh?' Les had a fair turn of words as ever, and we hot footed it as quickly as possible to the safety of the Britannia Club for the British Forces, which was a very posh NAAFI really. Behind the counter were three of the most glamorous Eastern beauties imaginable with no unsightly blue tattoos on their faces (as with all the other women we had seen outside). When I happened to remark on this to the English manager, he explained that they were all Christian Arab girls.

'Very nice too!' said Les with a certain look on his face.

'You've no chance, lad!' said the manager with a laugh as he went back to his office.

We did allow ourselves the dubious luxury of a forearm tattoo each—in a dingy little Arab shop where the bearded artist had a needle in a cork which he used to stab the ink into our cringing skin—wiping the blood off occasionally with the ends of his dirty, tattered burnous. (I still carry that tattoo depicting a Union Jack impaling a heart on my left forearm to this day.) One of the things I did purchase was a bright-red fez complete with black tassel as a souvenir of Egypt. The only comment about it from Les was 'I want a photo of you wearing that bloody thing sometime!' An event took place one evening which I always remember with amusement. Les and I decided to have a meal and entered a small but quite comfortable restaurant. We sat down to a tasty and very filling omelette, each accompanied by a small bottle of the local beer. As we were preparing to leave, Les said to the waiter, 'Is that your dad?' pointing to a large framed sepia photograph on the wall showing a corpulent man with a large moustache and wearing the ubiquitous Egyptian fez. The waiter looked startled.

'Oh no, effendi. That is His Majesty, our King Farouk!' he replied, and Les, unruffled as ever, came back with 'Well, I thought I'd ask cos you look a bit like him, but your belly's not as fat as yon bloke!' pointing to the photo. Trust my buddy to come up with some dry comment as always—bless him.

After the commanding officer had made a complaint to GHQ about the filthy old steamer we were having to board for the remainder of our journey up the coast to Haifa, we were embarked on this decrepit little one-funnel steamer. What an education! It had been almost sunk during the recent war when it was being used by the Italian Axis forces, and it showed. It carried a very unlikely title *The Eastern Prince* and was manned by a skipper who looked like Boris Karloff in a Sepia colour film, dozens of Chinese and Lascar seaman, and a very doubtful second officer in a torn vest and a Merchant Navy officer's cap. He was drunk as a skunk, which was evident as he swayed around the bow end shouting drunkenly 'Ankersh away, sirrr!'

Education indeed. There weren't enough hammocks to accommodate everyone, and a lot of us slept on the scruffy old mess tables, with our Board of Trade life jackets as pillows. The first night afloat, I woke to see the largest rat imaginable on a nearby mess table end, but as soon as it sensed my movement, it was away. Ugh!

The latrine arrangements were provided by a tarpaulin structure attached to the side of the ship, and inside was a long wooden plank with about ten bottom-sized holes. Several coarse toilet rolls were hung on string also. As we were perched over the side, the Mediterranean provided flushing needs! After I had made a needy visit with Les on the second morning, he turned to me and, with that semi-wise look of his, said, 'Have you noticed, Rod, the Lascars and Chinese don't go to the latrines when we are in there? They probably have a shitting shift!' Good old Les!

We had become so close since our nights in the Star in Windsor with Betty and Janet, and although he was a guardsman in the transport platoon and I was drummer in the Corps of Drums, we were as close as brothers.

CHAPTER 16

A UNIFORMED PRESENCE IN THE HOLY LAND!

WHEN THE BATTALION HAD been on active service in Palestine a few months, it was stationed in Camp 190 on the outskirts of Haifa, to the north on the road to Acre. The intervening period has been recalled and talked about many times over the years by myself to my family and anyone else who was willing to listen.

I still met Les occasionally in the NAAFI/EFI canteen for a pint, but not quite as often as I would have done had I known what was to come.

Attached to the battalion, we had a Greek Cypriot interpreter named Demetrios Demetriades. He held the honorary rank of sergeant, wearing a plain khaki BD with sergeants' chevrons on each arm to reinforce his official capacity, and acted as a battalion go-between with the Jews and the Arabs. He lived in a small village a few miles away from the camp and each day he was transported from his home and back again in one of our battalion half-track scout cars.

One day in April 1948, Les was the driver of the scout car and duly set off in the late afternoon with Sergeant Demetriades, accompanied by the battalion intelligence sergeant Joe Allan for the return journey, which normally took about two hours.

After four hours, when the vehicle had not returned to camp, a small party set off on the route to give help in case of a breakdown, although there had been no messages from Joe Allan to that effect. The search was fruitless, so the sequence of actions was initiated by the commanding officer and the Palestine police which resulted in a large search-and-rescue operation being launched overnight.

Early the next morning, the scout car was found eventually on the roadside near a small village. (That village position had no bearing on the matter though, as revealed by the Palestine police.) Poor old Demetriades was sitting in the co-driver's seat with his severed head in his lap and Sergeant Allan was laid in the back of the car with a wound in one leg and barely conscious. Of my buddy Les there was no sign, but relentless enquiries by the Palestine police led them eventually to a ditch covered over with a sheet of corrugated iron, where the bullet-riddled body of my dear old chum was lying face downwards in the bottom.

Passions ran high through the battalion and it took the combined actions of the commanding officer and the regimental sergeant major to prevent hordes of revenge-seeking grenadiers swanning off into the Judean Hills! The CO had the battalion drawn up in a square, and he spoke at some length to assure all the men that every action was being taken to seek out and bring the murderers to justice. The battalion padre then conducted a short act of devotion and prayers for our departed comrades and their loved ones. The camp resounded with the concluding roar of 'AMEN!' (There were quite a few tears here and there, mine among them.)

Our loss was believed to be the work of a small group of Haganah activists or the IZL, but that had yet to be established. Just to make sure that no one could break out of camp, a Staghound armoured car from our supporting resident RHA (Royal Horse Artillery) Chestnut Troop was placed across the camp gate. The perimeter wire was impregnable anyway with it's well-spaced, constantly manned, watchtowers.

Many years have passed since that incident, but every Remembrance Sunday, I place a small white cross and poppy, for my dear old buddy, in the Garden of Remembrance at Saint Paul's Parish Church near my home. This I do accompanied by a few moments of sad reflection and prayer.

April each year marks the anniversary or when I lost Les. I spend so many hours thinking of him- his warm, close friendship, broad accent, witty sayings, caustic comments with fools, and that wonderful broad grin and hearty laughter! I grow older with each passing year, but Les will be a teenager forever. On May 15 each year, I endeavour to don my Palestine tie bearing the Arab Dagger of Palestine Command, pin my Palestine Veterans and Forces Veterans badges in my blazer lapel, and remember Les with pride!

In May we began the preparations for our departure from Camp 190 and our withdrawal from Palestine. It seemed that a period of controlled chaos was to taking place while we disposed of those areas of stores and equipment which were considered as unnecessary for evacuation with the battalion but of a value to those who were to occupy the camp when we left. The six-pound anti-tank guns had their breech blocks removed and then tipped over the edge of a convenient wadi from a height that ensured their destruction, followed by some battalion trucks and half-track vehicles, including the cursed one which my buddy had driven to his death just weeks before.

One of the most moving moments in those hectic days of pre-embarkation was when it was decided that our camp chapel should not be left unguarded from desecration by those who followed, for they most certainly would have no Christians among their ranks. So, one morning, the drummers gathered in that lovely little pre-fabricated building which had been witness to our fairly adequate choral renditions for such a short time. It seemed so peaceful in the self-imposed silence as we gazed around at the stained and varnished wall cladding and the rows of folding chairs facing the beautiful little altar. When Major Rhys, our padre, arrived there were a few moments of prayer before he gave the instructions for 'firing' that place of Christian worship. We stacked all the chairs in the centre of the room, with the stripped altar forming the top of the pile, something symbolically defiant about that, perhaps? Then, after a careful emptying of a can of petrol everywhere in the floor area, the padre struck the fateful match and '*whoosh*'. Within moments, the chapel building was a blazing inferno, watched by us from a safe distance with a rather tearful padre at our side!

On 12 May, the battalion embarked on the Royal Navy cruiser HMS *Phoebe,* and a couple of other smaller Royal Navy vessels, which were waiting for us in Haifa harbour. We stood lining the rails to watch the ceremony taking place on the dockside. The King's Company was formed up as a guard of honour for the British High Commissioner as he read out the articles pertaining to the cessation of the British Mandate of Palestine and the withdrawal of the British forces. Then as the Union flag was lowered down one mast, the flag of the new State of Israel was raised on the other to flutter in the slight breeze, displaying in it's centre the Star of David for all to see. When the time came to weigh anchor and sail slowly from that accursed place, I let my gaze stray over in the direction of the war cemetery site, and I whispered a soft farewell to my dear old buddy Les, who was to remain there while I left for another place, not Blighty as we had all fondly imagined, but the North African desert country of Libya and the town of Tripoli, where we were destined to be stationed for another three years and five months!

In the period from 1945 to 1948, when the British mandate ended in Palestine, the British forces lost 785 men who were killed and had hundreds more wounded. Successive governments continue to this day to class that time of British Mandate in Palestine as a 'police action' and not therefore to be regarded as a war. I often wonder why that should be so, especially when I think of a grenadier's headstone in the Imperial War Graves cemetery on the Beach Road of Haifa in that land now known as Israel and a flat stone slab a few yards away bearing the name Demetrios Demetriades. That deployment in Palestine had all the ingredients of a war, as I remember, having lived through the six years of WWII—a war which had robbed millions of children of their childhood!

I was eighteen years of age at the time of leaving Palestine, but a fairly mature twenty-two when the battalion finally arrived back in England's exceptionally green and pleasant land, blissfully unaware that a dramatic time of royal duties was in the offing!

CHAPTER 17
GOOD FRIDAY IN NAZARETH

AS I TALK OF my recollections of my time in Palestine, thoughts take me back to a precious memory, seventy-two years ago, of Good Friday 1948.

The First Battalion Grenadier Guards was stationed in Camp 22d at Nathanya (now known as Netanya). The padre, Major Rhys, had arranged for the Corps of Drums to visit Nazareth and mark the holy day by attending a 'Stations of the Cross' service in the little Orthodox chapel there.

We all piled into the back of a Bedford QL three-tonner with Tom Cornall, our lance sergeant leading tipper, in the cab with the driver. I suppose the drum major, Swiv Petersen, thought it might be a nice chance to catch up with some office work (in his bunk, maybe?) so he remained in camp. That journey from the coast inland to Nazareth took us past many isolated Arab settlements which reminded me of the tracts I used to take home with me from Sunday school which often depicted scenes of the Holy Land in biblical times. Many of the houses looked to be constructed of mud, and there would be the ubiquitous burnous and white-robed figure standing on the roof to watch the solitary vehicle, as it passed by, laden with young British troops, as it growled and bumped across the endless dusty plains.

Eventually we started our climb up the zigzag road which led towards the heights of our destination. There was a hilarious incident as we crawled very slowly past a wheezing old lorry crawling up the same way and overflowing with tempting golden orbs of juicy jaffas. 'Drummers will be drummers', but before I draw a discreet curtain over the source of our unexpected refreshments en route I know one drummer of that time who could have gotten a job with any circus later on . . . juggling oranges with his legs astride a ten-foot drop!

Nazareth, once reached, revealed itself to be much as I had expected, a little cluster of white buildings clinging to a hillside. The little winding alleyways and streets were all dust, sand and a few sparsely covered patches of stone setts. There was just the odd patch of green here and there to relieve the stark whiteness of the village. I have often wished over the years that I could grow just one of those beautiful cedars of Lebanon in my garden, they are so redolent of the Eastern Mediterranean countries.

Before going to church, we visited the carpenter's shop where a padre, who had accompanied another small group of squaddies from another unit, gave a short talk about those days long ago when the boy Jesus worked as a carpenter in that very place with his father Joseph as his teacher. Standing there in that little bare room with whitewashed walls, I could almost hear Padre Denys Browning, my spiritual mentor at Pirbright, whispering in my ear ('You feel it don't you, Rodney?') and I did!

After the service in the chapel was over and we started making our way back to our truck for the journey back to Nathanya I realised I had left my small pack under my seat in the building. Without thinking what I was doing, I went galloping back on my own and retrieved it, only to feel the full wrath of Tom Cornall descend on me when I rejoined the group, as he very 'gently' reiterated the rigid rules of only going about in pairs with our rifles loaded with 'nine in the mag and one up the spout'! The rollicking was richly deserved, so I just stood there uttering the grenadiers' monosyllabic 'Sar'nt' of understanding as and when required. I bet our Lord never heard language like that in his days as a boy in Nazareth! (I wonder how they said 'stupid little sod' in Aramaic? LOL!) It was a wonderful spiritually uplifting day for me (Tom's rollicking not withstanding), and it has remained one of my more pleasant memories of our time in the Holy Land.

Two days later on Easter Sunday, we felt the other aspect of *our* existence in the land where Jesus and his disciples walked, as we were standing by, ready to move into Jerusalem! But that's another story!

CHAPTER 18

THE BUGLER OF MARETH

IN THE MIDDLE OF March 1949, the First Battalion Grenadier Guards was stationed in Gialo Barracks about four miles from Tripoli in Libya and I was now a corporal in the battalion Corps of Drums.

One morning I was summoned to the office of the senior major of the battalion, Major P. A. S. Robertson (of the marmalade manufacturing family). With some trepidation, I waited for him to come down the stairs from his sumptuous flat on the floor above. He was a man who liked his comforts, and I believe his accommodation was witness to this, although I never had the opportunity to visit his little den. After about ten minutes, he came into the office. He breezily waved to a chair, tapping his forehead casually in response to my salute.

'Oh, do sit down, corporal. Much too hot to stand on ceremony, what!' he said with a smile. Taking my cap off, I sat down in the easy chair in the corner of the small room and took the chance to have a closer look at the major as he picked up a red file and started to flick through some of the papers in it.

He was about five feet, ten inches in height, with a ruddy complexion, thinning sandy hair, and rather plump. But that was unremarkable when one considered his lifestyle, which was that of a man who liked the good things in life. He was more than generous with his hospitality too for any member of the battalion, of *any* rank, who happened to be in his company on any informal occasion and he ensured that there were plenty of those, if he had any opportunity to arrange one! He was extremely popular with every member of the battalion, and he would be sorely missed when he left the battalion a few months later to take command of the Third Battalion.

He seemed to take a particular interest in the Corps of Drums, often drifting into the barracks room during general practice. He would wave his hand dismissively when he saw that the drum major was about to stop the music and call us to attention, and would often stand there for a few minutes, tapping his cane against the palm of his hand in time to the beat.

The previous year, one afternoon during siesta, he had arrived outside the drums block in his jeep, with his servant at the wheel. After chatting with the drum major, he arranged for a party of about four of us to grab our swimming trunks and towels and join him for an afternoon trip to the forces' swimming beach on the outskirts of Tripoli. He was dressed in openwork sandals, a pale blue sun-suit, sunglasses, with the whole ensemble being topped off by a huge red straw sombrero! Quite a character was our loved Major PAS, and generous to a fault, as witnessed by the two crates of the local beer (Byrrh) which he had provided for his servant to dump in the sea close to the beach to keep cool for us. But underneath that casual and kind exterior was a very astute senior officer who was not to be crossed lightly or taken advantage of!

Putting the file down on his desk, he brought my attention back to him as he looked across at me and suddenly said, 'What do you know about Mareth, corporal?' I was taken aback for a moment. That was the last thing I had been expecting from the gallant major, but not to be seen wanting, I looked back into his unwavering blue-eyed stare and gave what I thought was his expected reply.

'It's in Tunisia, sir, and the site of one of our battles in the last war.'

He waved his hand airily and chuckled as he said. 'Yes, yes, but have you ever been there?' What a strange question, as if I had ever had the chance to visit that remote place way over to the west of our present location. Seeing the look on my face and sensing my obvious confusion, he went on to explain.

'Well, young fellow, me lad, you are going there now. Next week, in fact, in charge of four guardsmen. And taking your bugle with you too. What do you think to that?' He then explained in more detail that he had arranged to take a party of officers on a battlefield visit to Mareth March, which would coincide with the sixth anniversary of the battle where our Sixth Battalion took such a heavy toll of casualties at the infamous Horseshoe Ridge in March 1943. His own jeep would be driven by his guardsman servant, and the other four vehicles (which would include a fifteen-hundredweight truck for kit, etc.) would transport the party of officers. The major's jeep was also going to be the transport for yours truly! My duties would entail acting as the Non Comissioned Officer in charge (NCO i/n) of the five guardsmen (including Major Robertson's servant, for some reason) and sounding bugle calls including the 'Last Post' when we performed the small act of remembrance at the battle site cross.

When I got back to the Corps of Drums barracks room, I had to endure many jibes of 'Oooh! Look at the major's new boyfriend!' and such like. But it was all good-natured, for I knew that each and every one of my fellow drum NCOs would have changed places with me like a shot, given the chance to do so! Worse was to come from them when it leaked out that Major Robertson had specifically requested for me (by name) to accompany the expedition. 'It's cos he saw your lovely shaved legs during the battalion pantomime, I bet, Spot' (my nickname).

'I should keep your arse to the wall, mate!' was just one of the ribald remarks flying about during the few days before I scrambled thankfully into the back of the major's jeep. This he was driving, with his servant sat alongside. I felt rather exalted to be sat in the back of the lead vehicle as we led our little convoy through the barracks gate with the sentry giving a very snappy butt salute, which the major acknowledged with a casual wave of one hand, causing the jeep to do a small skitter in the sand piled outside the gate in the rutted roadway.

We drove along the Western Desert road leading from Tripolitania to the Tunisian frontier for about two hours before the major called for our first comfort halt. Together with the other guardsmen, I got out my haversack ration for the tiffin meal, which we ate sitting in the welcome shade of a burned-out German tank, one of many such heavier pieces of ironmongery that had proved impossible for the desert dwellers to confiscate! The el Senussi tribe seemed to hold firmly to their belief that if any article is left lying around with no visible owner, then Allah has provided it to them and they can take it for themselves without being regarded as klefty wallahs (thieves). I was glad that the major had decided to allow a more relaxed order of dress for our expedition, and we were all in KD (Khaki Drill) slacks and our desert chukka boots instead of the usual obligatory shorts, leather boots, webbing anklets, and hose tops. These would have resulted in a few badly sunburned knees by now, as borne out by some sore necks (even though deeply tanned after our first twelve months in the searing heat of Libya). Fortunately, we also had our KD shirtsleeves rolled down for the journey through the Western Desert and were protected as much as possible from the unremitting heat. As an added precaution against the all-pervading clouds of dust whipped up by the wheels of our vehicles, we all wore a pair of A/Gas goggles from our respirator packs, leaving the pack in barracks.

Before resuming our journey, we took the opportunity to dot our i's and cross our t's in the desert sand. It was a common fact, though, that in the heat of the desert (probably due to perspiration evaporation), we didn't have the need to pass water as much as would be the case elsewhere. Probably as well too, for our leader didn't believe in calling for many halts on the journey. It was strange for me as I sat thinking in the back of the jeep whilst surveying mile after mile of knocked-out tanks, scorched trucks and 88 mm guns pointing drunkenly in all directions, that only a few years before, my dad had probably driven his truck along this same road as a RASC driver with the British Fifth Army in 1944, before crossing over to Sicily then Italy and then pushing up to where he was finally demobbed in Naples.

After a few more hours bumping along the seemingly interminable desert highway, we passed the large roadside sign indicating that we were now in Tunisia, and the distant horizon began to reveal this new country to be one of mountains in plenty!

After a couple of hours, we entered a small Arab town called Medenine where Major Roberson dismounted and was soon in animated conversation in fluent French with a small Arab who was clad from head to feet in a rather grubby djellaba after emerging from a whitewashed building — one of a dozen or so at the side of the main street. I heard the words 'Caserne Francais — aywah!' in a mixture of French and Arabic patois as the man waved in an affirmative manner towards the foothills on our left, which seemed to soar skywards, with no sign of the French barracks that he was alluding to! With a casual wave of his hand and a shout of 'Merci. Shukkarah!' our major thanked the little Arab official who, it seemed, was the town councillor of sorts who had been appointed by the French Colonial Office to administer the little town and its population — though there was no one around other than the said official!

We seemed to climb for hours along the narrow winding dusty road, alongside the Wadi Zigzaon, ever upwards on whatever apparently fruitless goose chase we had been sent by the seedy little town clerk back in Medenine. When it seemed that we would have to call a halt, if only to let the swirling clouds of choking dust settle, and to take a reluctant but necessary drink of warm chemically treated water from our water bottles, we rounded a bend to see the tricolour of France hanging limply atop a gleaming white flag post, quickly followed by the sight of a white-and-red banded traffic barrier across the road as it gave access to a large camp of white barracks huts. As we drew to a halt at the barrier, we could see that there were about twenty or so of these huts forming the four sides of a large sandy parade ground. The perimeter boundary of the camp consisted of a formidable 'triple cat wire' barbed wire fence. (No breaking out of that camp at night then!)

When Major PAS dismounted and approached the small white hut at the side of the barrier, he was met by a very large uniformed soldier wearing the white kepi of the French Foreign Legion and an exceptionally smart starched and almost-white uniform of shirt and sharply creased trousers, which were tucked into white gaiters buttoned to just below his knees. Across his chest was a tangle of cords from a huge Scarlet Aguilette, and the butt of a business-like revolver was visible in the blancoed holster and belt at his waist. Standing about ten paces beyond the *gendarme militaire sous-officier* — (for such he proved to be!) just inside the camp was his slightly shorter *caporal*, seemingly bored by our presence, but carrying a small sub-machine gun at the ready! Both of the French NCOs were wearing the black brassards of Les Gendarmerie Militaire Francais.

As the major and the French sergeant conversed, we became aware of straggling bunches of men in a multitude of uniforms approaching the wire to gaze with interest at their unusual visitors. I noticed the white caps and blue pom-poms of a few French matelots dotted here and there in the crowd of curious soldats, but there were three common identifying features about them all. Their heads were shaved down to the skull, they had clogs on their feet instead of boots, and all were wearing a khaki overall jacket which had on the left breast a large black letter *P*. I noticed it was repeated in much larger capitals on the backs of all the men when they turned to shuffle and clatter away back across the parade ground towards the huts in response to the shouted commands from the corporal with the machine gun.

After about ten minutes of conversation between our major and the French sergeant, there was a sharp command from the latter, and both the NCOs snapped to attention while the taller of the men cut off a crisp French-style salute and gave a smiling remark that sounded something like 'Tres plaiser, mon capitan,' as Major PAS waved in his usual airy fashion and ambled back to the jeep. Perhaps the French NCO didn't know that a British officer with a crown on his shoulder was above the rank of captain? It transpired that instead of arriving at our required destination, we had made an unexpected visit to the French colonial armed forces penal battalion, at a place called Tataouine, which necessitated turning round for a return journey back down to Medenine to pick up the correct route to our required destination, the town of Gabes, further up the Tunisian coast!

Probably an officer other than our easy-going Major Robertson would have been raving about the inconvenience and extra four hours travelling time added to our journey because of the faulty topographical knowledge of the Arab town clerk of Medenine. However, he just took it in his stride and indeed seemed to be amused by the comedy of errors that had almost resulted in a party of officers and other ranks of the Grenadier Guards spending the night as guests of a French penal battalion in the wastes of Tunisia, and I suspect that he embellished the tale over dinner in the officers' mess on our return to the battalion!

There were two French/Arab towns of any significance on the Tunisian coast at that time, just after WWII. One was Sfax and the other, higher up the coast, was Gabes. This is where we were to be billeted for the next couple of days, after we eventually arrived at our correct destination at the barracks of the Fourth Chasseurs D'Afrique, a regiment of French colonial soldats under the command of French officers and senior *sous-officiers*.

We were given a warm welcome by the French commanding officer and some half a dozen other officers and a chap with a rigid backbone, bristling moustache, and a gold-embroidered kepi, whom I took to be their equivalent of our sergeant major. The officers dispersed to the officers' mess for the night, and the sergeant major conducted myself and the guardsmen driver/servants to the barracks hospital where we would be accommodated for the two nights of our stay. It was considered to be more fitting for men of a British Foot Guards regiment to be entertained and fed there rather than in one of the barracks rooms, a decision with which I agreed after getting the opportunity later on to visit one of the long seemingly airless rooms where the colonial troops lived!

I had been briefed by Major Robertson about the arrangements for our visit to the Mareth battlefield the following day, and we were left to amuse ourselves for the evening after our meal. This was basic but sufficient enough to satisfy our hunger. It had been cooked for us in the hospital kitchen, and we sat down to eat at a table in a little side ward, where we were looked after by a small French medical orderly, designated to be our man for the duration of our stay. I can't remember his correct name after all these years, so I will just refer to him by the name given to him by the guardsmen, who assumed that all Frenchmen were called Pepe for some reason!

Pepe was a pleasant little man who was determined to make us comfortable and anticipated our needs in advance, if possible. We all wished he had left the tea-making to us, however. His offering was an experience not to be repeated by any members of the tea-drinking race! Poor old Pepe had tried to make tea in the same way that he would have made coffee, the everyday beverage (together with the rough red wine) of the French soldier, in that he had boiled the tea leaves in a saucepan! The resulting brew was quite out of this world. Of course, there was no milk to make the vicious brown liquid a little more palatable, but there was no way that we were going to abuse the little orderly's efforts on our behalf, so we heaped more sugar than usual in the big white drinking bowls and bravely drank every drop. I could see that Pepe was extremely grateful when Guardsman Rawlings offered to make the tea, if Pepe wished, while we were there!

The hospital beds looked invitingly comfortable and promised the chance of a well-earned rest after our long journey along the Western Desert highway, but we were men with a thirst above all other things. We made our way gladly to the small building just outside the barracks gate, to which Pepe directed us, and which we assumed to be the French army's equivalent of our NAAFI. It appeared to be brightly lit after the rather dim barracks lighting, and there was a string of fairy lights around the arched doorway.

It was reasonably quiet inside the large room we entered, and we assumed it was one of the nights when our French friends were feeling the midweek pinch that is the lot of all soldiers between paydays. The centre of the room formed a small dance floor, the music for dancing being provided presumably by a large jukebox in the corner of the room, from which drifted the soft tones of the

French Bing Crosby, Charles Trenet. There were several alcoves and banquettes around the room, which gave it a rather crowded appearance, and the promise of rather rowdy nights when the soldats got their meagre pay! There were a couple of curtained doorways, which led presumably to the toilets and staff quarters etc., while the corner of the room was taken up by a small but very well-stocked bar. This was concluded from seeing the large amount of gaily coloured bottles on the racks behind the attractive barmaid, who was leaning on the bar counter with her arms crossed in front of a well-padded bosom. She was talking quietly and laughing with the two military policemen standing each with a foot on the footrail, holding glasses of beer. I noticed that their kepis were to hand on their bar stools, presumably ready to don quickly if needed for any reason.

Both the barmaid and the MPs gave us a warm welcome in French, and after purchasing a couple of bottles each of the local beer, we made our way over to an alcove near the jukebox. I had a fleeting memory of the last time I sat near one, singing with Les in the Star back in Windsor. I was pulled out of my reverie by the soft swish of the curtain nearest our seats as a rather pretty young girl entered the room and made her way over to where we sat gazing at her with undisguised admiration. We didn't get too close to the girls in Tripoli, where the local Italian parents and duennas were still smarting from the non-frat ban they had to contend with until just a couple of months before we landed from Palestine the previous year. If we made as if to speak or even smile at any of the young signorinas, they were quickly ushered out of our way with whispers of something like 'Basta! Basta!' etc. and glances of disdain in our direction from their escorts.

When the young mademoiselle arrived at our table, she said something in French and smiled invitingly as she gestured towards the curtained doorway, and that was when I realised that we were sitting in a French military bordello, and not their version of our NAAFI as we had thought previously! The guardsmen looked towards me with questioning looks on every face. Did they expect me to lead the way into the back parlour, for goodness' sake? Nothing would persuade me to display the slightest indication of any interest in the activities of those back rooms, and I felt my whole body start to weld itself to the safe bastion of my seat!

'You please yourselves,' I said softly, 'but there is no way that I am going to follow her through that bloody doorway!' I picked up one of my empty bottles as if to emphasise my preference for another round of drinks.

'Well, you can please yourself, corporal, but I'm gonna have two pennorth of whatever she's got. She's a corker,' said Rawlings as he got to his feet, took the girl's hand, and allowed himself to be led through the curtains to whatever was provided beyond that doorway!

It was quite evident after a while that Whitehead, who was the only one of our little gang likely to follow Rawlings and the girl through the curtain, had decided to stick with us as we got on with the serious business of the night: slaking the thirst caused by the desert dust on our tonsils. About twenty minutes later, we were rejoined by Romeo Rawlings with a satisfied grin on his face. He sat down and immediately picked up a bottle, emptying it down his throat at one go! He then sat smirking until curiosity provoked one of his companions, Whitehead (of course!), to come out with, 'Well, what happened like?'

'Oh, it were great, mate,' said Rawlings, warming to the pleasant task of revealing his recent activities in every gory detail. 'She told me to take me trousers off, and me drawers like. Then she took me over to t'sink and started washing me old man. Then she said, "Eengleesh, jonny?" flashing 'er eyes like.'

Another of our company then said with a snort, 'Well, that were obvious weren't it, with your British KD and cap badge, I should have thought. What did you tell 'er?' At which, Rawlings looked at him with a grin and replied slowly, 'Well, what could I say to a question like that except "Every inch, luv! Every inch!"' At this, we all erupted into roars of laughter and promptly got another round in as we settled back to hear the rest of his story!

The next morning, we all woke to find the table in the centre of the little hospital ward had been set out with chairs along both sides, and our dinking bowls were sat at each place, together with an enamel plate. In the centre of the table were some big basketwork trays on which were sat large crusty bread buns, rashers of some streaky-looking meat (probably horsemeat, but we weren't going to ask!), and huge slices of cheese with big holes in it, which smelled like dirty socks but turned out to be quite palatable. Pepe was waiting patiently to show Rawlings where they could go to prepare the tea, and soon he returned with a huge canteen full of the steaming beverage that we were all ready for after the drinking session of the previous night. Pepe indicated that the large enamel pitcher in the centre of the table contained the rough red wine that the French military had with every meal, and there were a number of small thick glasses for our convenience. It was quite obvious that Pepe had gone to a great deal of effort to try and make our stay as comfortable as possible, and we were going to miss him when we left.

The rest of the day was devoted to carrying out the duty for which we had travelled all those dusty miles from Tripoli, and we were soon bumping our way again along the Tunisian road, out to the site of the Battle of Mareth which had taken place just six years ago on that day, 16 March. I kept giving my bugle totally unnecessary rubs with the yellow duster which I had kept on one side for the purpose of presenting a spotless, gleaming instrument when it came to the sounding of my call later on.

Eventually we dismounted at the Mareth Battlefield, and after a quick glance at our surroundings, we formed a semi-circle facing across the large valley or wadi. Major Robertson began to describe the battle on that site, which had been the destination for the Sixth Battalion of our regiment after driving in convoy nearly three thousand miles along the dusty roads from Syria to boost the British forces (including our sister regiment, the Coldstream Guards) attempting to smash a way through the German Mareth Line.

I looked across to where I could see the wreck of a burned out Bren Carrier over on one of the slopes, wondering if it was one of the Sixth Battalion vehicles. But the lasting impression of the afternoon here was the incredible silence, broken only by the soft, reverential tones of the major as he described in vivid detail how the battalion had stumbled into a minefield under the commanding heights of the ridge above named the Horseshoe Ridge, which caused the ensuing battle to be ever after known as the Horseshoe Battle. The battalion took heavy losses that night, suffering over 260 casualties, including 77 killed (14 of the 24 officers, and 63 other ranks).

After Major Robertson finished his moving talk, there were many questions obviously from us all, and I for one would remember forever our Sixth Battalion with pride and a lasting awareness of the terrible losses inflicted on our regiment in just one terrible night of the North African campaign, only a few short years previously on the very ground where I was standing!

Soon the party formed up in a single rank, with Major Robertson standing in front and myself out on my own at the side of the simple stone cross which had been made from local stone by the pioneer platoon of the battalion after the battle to stand with the crosses of the fallen grenadiers, but was now a lone reminder, because the bodies were later moved to the large war cemetery near the town of Sfax.

The major called our little party to attention, and on our behalf and that of thousands of other grenadiers (past and serving) throughout the world, he delivered the homily . . .

They shall grow not old, as we that are left grow old,
age shall not weary them, nor the years condemn.
At the going down of the sun, and in the morning,
we will remember them!
And we all responded with 'We *will* remember them!'

Bringing my bugle smartly up to my mouth, I said a silent prayer that I would not muff it, and started to sound 'Last Post', gazing as I did so across the sweep of the valley to the wreck of the burned-out carrier and trying to ignore the stinging in my eyes as the tears trickled down my cheek. I was determined to pay my own proud tribute to my fallen comrades, concentrating on every note of my call so that it rang out crystal clear, without a single cracked note all the way through to the last echoing E which gradually faded away to its destination in the hills. After that, I wasn't going to cheapen my performance with the usual humdrum 'Rouse' used for reveille in barracks. I took the opportunity to round off with the 'Long Reveille', knowing that the party would appreciate that rather grand but tricky tribute, and again I managed to produce a faultless brassy bugle call!

'Well done, corporal,' said Major Robertson, tactfully ignoring my tear-stained cheeks as we got back in to our vehicles for the return to the French barracks in Gabes.

We had a few more drinks in the bar that night, but there were to be no more excursions to the nether regions. The conversation being devoted in the main to the events of the day and the lasting impression it had left on all of us, together with a renewed sense of pride in our great regiment. It was mixed with sadness too for our fallen comrades of the old Sixth Battalion now lying in the peace of the war cemetery in Sfax.

The remainder of the stay with our French hosts flew after that, and in no time at all, or so it seemed, we were back with our First Battalion in Tripoli, full of tales to tell of Major Robertson's expedition to honour the memory of the Sixth Battalion in Mareth. I bet Rawlings had a tale of his own to add too!

It is many years now since I sounded the bugle at Mareth in March 1949, but the memory remains crystal clear, and whenever I have occasion to visit Wellington Barracks, I gaze at the cross in its present location near the Guards chapel. In my mind, I am once again the nineteen-year-old bugler of Mareth, sending those calls resounding across the desolate hills of Tunisia.

Footnote

Over the years, the simple stone cross became ravaged by the winds and sands of Tunisia, so a decision was made to remove it to a place in England where it could be cared for. It stood at the Guards

Depot at Caterham until the depot's closure. Then it was moved to the new Guards Depot at Pirbright, but when those barracks became the base for the army training regiment, the cross was moved yet again to its present location opposite the main door of the Guards Chapel in London, where it is cared for by the London branch of the Grenadier Guards Association. Each year, on the occasion of the Regimental Remembrance Sunday, the dwindling few veterans of the Sixth Battalion gather at the cross to say a prayer for their fallen comrades of the Sixth Battalion and lay a wreath at the base.

CHAPTER 19
HOW THE FIFTIES
STARTED FOR ME

THE YEAR 1949 WENT out with a bang and the sound of the fireworks drifting over the eight miles or so, 'as the vulture flies', between the city of Tripoli and our station of Prinn Barracks out on the edge of the Libyan desert. The sky was lit up for nearly twenty minutes, and it was a great sight for the sergeants' mess members of the First Battalion Grenadier Guards who congregated in the patio garden. There was much back-slapping, hand-shaking and even a few kisses too in some cases, for quite a few of the 'married pads' had twisted the arm of the master technical sergeant, my old pal Harold 'Tex' Howarth, into laying on a couple of three-tonners to ferry them and their ladies out from their married quarters in Azzizia and Tripoli City for the evening's festivities. I didn't see much of this as I was, of course, at my usual place on the piano stool ('Just for the evening OK?' from the sergeant major), and the night ended about 03.30 hours on 1 January 1950, a long evening for my fingers, as it seemed that everyone had remembered a long-forgotten song that he, she, or they wished to sing for the entertainment of their sympathetic friends!

As I came out of the mess eventually, I stood for a while by the patio fishpond, which was very cleverly illuminated from below the water line, thanks to the ingenuity of a very artistic lance sergeant in the pioneer platoon, Doug Ashfield. Floating on the water were several pieces of bread, lettuce, something which looked suspiciously like a pair of 'drawers hallelujah!' (cellular tropical underpants), and a dead goldfish floating upside down. Poor thing, he would never know that today was the first day of a new year *and* a new decade, the fifties!

Further to the music theme, I had a couple of small parts in the battalion variety show *'It Serves You Right!'*, which was proving to be such a success that it went on tour all along the Tripolitania and Cyrenaica coast garrisons, playing to full houses in every case (well, they had nothing else to do had they?). In one act, I was in the full dress of an Arab of the El-Senussi tribe (they lent us the costumes with a good show of friendliness) in the scenario put on by the Corps of Drums, who were all similarly robed, and I sang 'On the Road to Mandalay', a particular favourite of mine (if it was sung by Peter Dawson!). Another part called for me to play the part of a gangster's moll, after which I swore that never again would anyone get me to shave my legs! All great fun and very therapeutic for a battalion, which was just starting to get a touch of the doolallies after a couple of years in the North African heat! Even our sergeant major (the popular Les Burrell) was involved as head of the make-up department. Great times!

In June we took part in the King's Birthday Parade on the large sandy area lying between the Tripoli Promenade (Il Lungomare) and the harbour itself, ourselves finding the escort for the Colour and Number 2 Guard. The whole proceedings were overshadowed by the wreck of a huge steamer lying on its side in the water of the port where Allied bombers had sunk it for carrying the Red Cross as a hospital ship while acting as a German troop carrier for the Afrika Korps.

Speaking of the Afrika Korps, by the way, we had a transport company attached to the division manned entirely by POWs of the

Afrika Korps. They were great blokes and I shared many a pint with them down in Tripoli City, listening to them singing their lieder! When the troopship carrying repatriated German ex-POWs called into Tripoli on its way back to Germany, quite a large crowd of British service personnel gathered on the quayside to wave the boat off as it sailed away. It was carrying a couple of thousand waving bronzed German ex-servicemen lining the ship's rails and singing, who, after years of desert warfare and imprisonment, were returning back to their loved ones and homeland at last!

Taking part with us in the Birthday Parade were another four guards found by the Third Battalion Coldstream Guards and the First Battalion Queen's Own Cameron Highlanders. Music for the parade was provided by the two Guards Corps of Drums; the Band, Pipes, and Drums of the Camerons; and the military band of our divisional armoured regiment, the Fourth and Seventh Dragoon Guards. Of course, we were in khaki drill slacks and shirts as we couldn't have worn tunics and bearskins in that searing heat, even if we had been in possession of such items. When we had left Blighty in early 1948 and were still khaki grenadiers—our introduction to Home Service clothing was yet to come, when we got back to Blighty in late 1951!

On the conclusion of the King's Birthday Parade, we were transported back to our barracks, sitting or standing and swaying, as we held on to the canopy rails of the three-tonners, no canopies of course, due to the heat. For some odd reason, we had a few Coldstream drummers on our truck, which was fortunate as I was able to witness the birth of a little piece of Coldstream folklore on the journey back to the Coldstream Barracks as a detour while en-route to our own.

There were two cinemas in Tripoli: our own AKC cinema—which, unusually, was not known as the Globe but as Miramare (Seaview)—and the Italian one, 'Il Kino'. As the truck passed by the Italian place of entertainment, one of the Coldstreamers, a certain Drum Lance Sergeant Carter, suddenly called out to all within earshot in a broad scouse accent and no one missed what he said.

'Hey, look, lads, at what's on tonight . . . *Oggi*—funny name for a film, heh?' And so was born Oggy Carter, too late to retract his bit of information, as all those with a smattering of Italian told him that *oggi* meant 'today'! The nickname Oggy stayed with him throughout his service, and a few years later, when we were both drum majors in London, the garrison sergeant major (RSM George 'Micky' Stone, Irish Guards) had a good old laugh as, accompanied by Oggy's grins, the other four drum majors taking part in the 1958 Queen's Birthday Parade told him the tale during a tea break one day as we attended the usual one week drum major's refresher training with him in preparation for our centre stage roles on the parade. Oggy and I were great buddies though (as all the Guards drum majors were), and I made a special point of sending a goodwill message to him when I left my own regiment in 1960. I hope he received it.

In July, I was really lucky as my family raised the cost of my airfare so I could fly home for four weeks leave in Blighty as a twenty-first birthday present, although I couldn't fly until a few days after that date, owing to the air charter flight schedules. A wonderful surprise as it cost them £50 for my return flight (a lot of money at the time) with a company called Airwork Limited based at Blackbushe Airport in the south of England. They had done the same for me the previous year too, so my fellow sergeants, in the mess generally, and the Corps of Drums in particular, made jokes about the few of us going on 'these annual trips to Blighty.' But it was all good-natured, and they would all have willingly gone in our place given the opportunity, I think. We had to stay overnight with RAF Castel Benito a few miles from Tripoli (the RAF base would become Tripoli Airport in later years) so that we were there for the early morning checking-in procedures and our take-off at 08.00 hours. Although I had made the same journey only twelve months before, I felt as nervous as if it were to be that first time in my life that I had taken to the skies. It was with the same white knuckles that I sat strapped in my seat for the take-off! The aircraft was a small twin-engined Vickers Viking, holding two crew and fifty passengers, including the cabin stewardess, who sensed that I was uneasy in flight and gave me a handful of sweets to suck on. They also demonstrated how to alleviate the popping pain in my ears, no such thing as pressurised cabins then of course, by pressing my ears and swallowing. It helped a little but I still had a certain amount of pain for a couple of days after we landed in England.

The total mileage of the journey from Tripoli was about three thousand miles. This was *not* as the crow flies as we had to make slight detours from the flight path in order to refuel at Tunis and Nice! We had to put our watches back one hour to accommodate BST as we approached Blackbushe airport. Taking the new time into account, I worked out that the whole flight had taken just over nine hours, as it was 16.15 local time as we landed, not bad! After going through the customs hut, I was soon sat on the coach which would take us to the BOAC airways terminal in Victoria, a journey of just over an hour, during which I sat wondering at the greenery everywhere I looked outside the windows. It had been just over a year since my last leave and I had become acclimatised again to date palms, sandy landscapes, and white buildings, so the soft ethos of my lovely homeland welcome was just as wonderful as it had been the last time.

The coach drew into the front of the air terminal and glancing up at the huge clock on the white tower with its flapping flag, I saw that I had about two hours in which to make my way to King's Cross and catch my train to my home city of Leeds. I practically ran up Buckingham Palace Road to Victoria Station to travel on the Tube to the main London station of LNER and my journey north on, I hoped, the *Flying Scotsman* (boyhood dreams again!). The flight from Tripoli to England had taken nine hours, and I reckoned that the entire journey from Blackbushe to my home in Yorkshire by coach, Tube, and steam train took just over twelve hours, for the clock at Wellington Street (Leeds Central) station was showing 04.25 hours as I walked along the platform, giving a weary grin to the driver and his fireman standing on the footplate of the hissing locomotive and their good-natured shout of 'Get your knees, brown lad!' Most folks at the time recognised the white arrowhead formation patch on my sleeve, associating it with troops serving in the Middle East, and I was deeply tanned anyway, so they were only joking! I forgot to look at the nameplate on the side of the green locomotive as I was in a hurry to get out and catch a tram home, it could have been the the *Flying Scotsman* of my dreams but I will never know now.

I had a most wonderful leave with all my family and those friends who were not away in the forces themselves. Four weeks passed all too quickly and I was soon back in Tripoli to be met with the news that in two days' time I would be on my travels again, as we were going to sail across the Med to Malta GC on a big defence exercise. It was only a few short years ago since this little island had been under siege at sea by U-boats attacking its supply convoys and under constant attack from the air by German bombers based only a few flying miles away on Sicily. The war story of Malta is well-documented, but I must make reference to the fact that His Majesty the King had declared that all the people of Malta had undergone so much personal experience of frontline warfare and endured so many hardships that it was impossible to identify individuals who had experienced more than their neighbour, so he decided that the whole island itself would be decorated with the highest civilian decoration possible, the one he had instituted in place of the Albert Medal, the George Cross. Henceforth, Malta would be entitled to be called the Island of Malta GC.

There was a strong Royal Navy presence in the Middle East at the time and the Mediterranean Fleet was based in Malta, so it was no surprise to find ourselves sailing to the island from Tripoli on the cruiser HMS *Eurylaus*. This was a large warship quite capable of carrying all the battalion personnel designated to take part in DXM (Defence Exercise Malta), even though it entailed the Corps of Drums sleeping out on the decking of the ship's holy of holies— the quarterdeck!

This was our second experience of life aboard a cruiser of the Med Fleet, as we had previously embarked on another, HMS *Phoebe*, when we left Palestine over two years before when it became Israel.

We had an overnight trip over the reasonably short distance from the coast of North Africa to Malta, and even now seventy years later, I remember the magic of lying on the quarterdeck, hearing the faint swish of the bow ploughing its way through the balmy Mediterranean night and looking up at the moonlit sky with it's myriad of twinkling stars. Music was relayed throughout the ship on the PA system and I always associate the song 'La Mer', sung by Charles Trenet, with my memories of that magical night at sea on HMS *Euryalus*.

We were accommodated in Saint George's Barracks for our stay on Malta, and if you were to ask any member of the battalion (at the time) for any particular memory, it would be the salt water! As a result of the constant bombing raids during the wartime siege, the fresh water network of the island had cracked, allowing a contamination by the surrounding seawater. Although work was in progress to put things to right, at that particular time in 1950, the drinking water was very salty. For a couple of days, it was a common sight in the mess to see wry faces in the dining room as cups of tea were quickly put down on the table after the slightest sip! So, salty water was exchanged for the tang of chemically treated water from the battalion water bowsers, not the most pleasant alternative!

Our role on DXM was to establish a strong defensive position for the purpose of repelling a proposed sea-borne landing and invasion by units of the United States Marines Corps. We spent a couple of days labouring under the punishing glare of the subtropical sun preparing shell scrapes and erecting sangars with the many boulders to be found in abundance in the inhospitable Maltese countryside. It was virtually an impossible task to dig any slit trenches, the ground was far too hard and rocky.

When the day dawned for the planned 'invasion' from the sea, we stood to in our strongly fortified positions in the rural areas around the city of Valetta, reinforced by all the guns of the Malta Coastal Artillery trained seawards. The minutes turned to hours, and word filtered through to us in our positions that two large freighters or troopships had been sighted. However, instead of heaving to and lowering away their assault craft, they kept on course and vanished into the distant east—had we frightened them off? We were eventually stood down and transported back to barracks where we were given the news that, thousands of miles away in Korea, units of the Chinese Communist army had crossed the thirty-eighth parallel from North Korea. This violated the sovereignty of the South, resulting in our 'enemy' American Marines now being en route to the aid of the country of South Korea, and a war which would also involve Great Britain.

Because our stay in Malta had been planned to last for ten days, we found ourselves with the unexpected pleasures of plenty of walking-out leave into Valetta, and it was there that another large slice of my education was obtained. Running down from the square in Valetta to the docks was a long and narrow sloping street which descended in stepped intervals throughout it's length with dozens of bars on either side. The street was notorious with men of the armed forces generally, and seamen of the world in particular. It's correct name was Straight Street, but it was more commonly referred to as the Gut! The bars were drinking dens really, some with upstairs dance rooms populated by hostesses where visiting servicemen were invited to dance in exchange for a drink. The drink was invariably a small glass of coloured water, but supposedly gin or whisky, etc. for which the unwitting customer would pay an exorbitant sum and find himself paying 5d. (2p) for his bottle of Blue Anchor beer, plus about 3s. (15p) for the small glass of coloured water.

I was sat upstairs in the dance hall of a bar called the New Life with another two drum sergeants, namely Tom Cornall and John Tilbury, when one of these painted harridans came to our table and said to Tom, 'You buy me a drink, johnny?'. Tom replied that he would be pleased to buy the young lady a beer the same as he was drinking. That was not what she was in business for, of course, because those little glasses of coloured water represented clear profit for the owners. So, she persisted with another 'No, no, johnny. No beer for me. You buy me a gin, please?' only to get the same rejoinder from Tom that he would buy her a beer same as he was drinking.

So, after a few seconds of pouting her lips and pleading, she realised it was no go with Tom. The scenario suddenly changed as, with a quick flick of her skirt, she put a hand into her pants and withdrew it again, holding a couple of pubic hairs in her fingers which she dropped into Tom's glass. With a snarling Cockney accent, she said to him, 'Right then, you tight bastard, drink my health with that!' She stomped off to another table, resuming her wheedling with a group of French matelots, leaving Tom dumbfounded, me with a look of shock on my face, and John in fits of uncontrollable giggling!

Oh yes, my education widened greatly and memorably in Malta, for the following evening, we went to another part of Malta known as Floriana, where 'girls' of a different type were to be found, many with Adam's apples and five o'clock shadows.

We went into a large bar and dance hall known as the Klondyke Kabin. There was a staircase leading down from street level to the bar and dance hall, and the first thing I spotted was a 'girl' lounging against the wall at the foot of the stairs, cleaning under her fingernails with the point of a very nasty-looking stiletto! When we got into the dance hall, we found that the dancing had paused for a solo spot by the pianist. I was enthralled to hear 'The Dream of Olwen' played most beautifully by the legend of the Floriana bars, Minco, and it was he/she who managed the Klondyke with his/her partner 'Bobbie' (the one with the stiletto).

The dance music that night was brilliant, and our day ended with Tom and me dragging our small buddy John away from his partner and off the floor as we left. John was saying drunkenly, 'Lift me up, fellers. I want to kiss her goodnight.'

Tom said to him in soothing tones, 'You can't, John, because she's a bloke!'

Another evening found me stood on a table in the Duke of Kent's Bar, pouring all I had into singing 'My Foolish Heart' to a bevy of cooing, sighing beauties, female this time but still ladies of the night!

My lasting and most beautiful memory of my stay in Malta was my short relationship with a very pretty Petty Officer Wren, whom I met in one of the pukka dance halls. We must have danced together for two or three hours, me a Guards sergeant in army KD, and her in a most fetching white skirt and open-necked tunic shirt with the crossed blue anchors and crown of a petty officer on her sleeve. She was light as a feather in my arms, with short blonde curls that rested on my chest in the smoochy numbers and gorgeous blue eyes which she kept flashing at me as she gave me one of her infectious giggles.

It was she who taught me to kiss gently, not like a bruiser, and on our last night together she took me into the Guards Office at the Wrens quarters in Valetta to be introduced to her best friend, a chief PO Wren. It was there that I saw, for the only time in my life, a Guards commander knitting baby garments! It transpired that she had a little grandson back in Blighty and she passed her time knitting little things for him — sweet! I left my petty officer Wren in Malta. The last I saw of her was as she stood, where we had embraced and kissed our farewells on our last night together, at our prearranged spot on the grand harbour walls as the *Euryalus* steamed away, with us lining the rails and hundreds of the girls of Malta shouting and waving. I don't know if she could pick me out, but I could certainly see her as she stood there with her CPO friend's arm round her shoulder. Even from that fairly long distance, I could see that she was weeping. We exchanged letters—just once, after that parting, and I often wonder if she remembered me with affection over the years? I have never forgotten her, or her name, but that remains my secret and I will never divulge it even if you were to ask! My hope for her is that she has had a happy fruitful life and is living quietly in contented retirement somewhere in this wide world.

That eventful year of 1950 was to end for me with one of the most memorable occasions ever, and one which I would refer to many, many times over the ensuing years: a royal visit!

It was decided that in early December, our colonel, Her Royal Highness the Princess Elizabeth, would visit the battalion together with her sister Her Royal Highness the Princess Margaret Rose. They would be accompanied by the famous grenadier Field Marshall Boy Browning, of '*A Bridge Too Far*' fame, and a former captain and adjutant of the battalion in pre-war Egypt. I was half hoping that the field marshall would be accompanied by his wife. What a feather in my cap if I could ask Daphne du Maurier for her autograph and get it for my mum, one of her most avid readers! It was not to be, however, as the field marshall travelled out to the Middle East on his own for the visit.

At the time, our colonel and her husband, HRH Prince Philip, were living in a villa in Malta where Prince Philip was serving as a lieutenant commander in the Mediterannean Fleet and commanding the frigate HMS *Magpie*. Prince Philip's uncle, Admiral the Lord Louis Mountbatten, was commander-in-chief of the Med Fleet and his flag was on the cruiser HMS *Liverpool*.

During the run-up, there were many battalion parades, and we were well schooled in the protocol to be observed if spoken to by our royal visitor. 'Your Royal Highness' when answering for the first time, and 'Mam' as in jam (*not* 'Ma'am') after that. The commanding officer accompanied the senior major for the dummy runs (the major acting as Princess Elizabeth!). All went smoothly eventually, and we were all geared up and ready to roll on the great day. But fate intervened, and we were blessed by one of our local sandstorms. Known as ghiblis in Libya and khamsin in other parts of North Africa, they blow for several days, with the air filling with brown haze, and an accompanying fine gritty sand which permeated just everywhere. Even the food in the mess had the bonus of extra grit in the sandwiches, just what brawny grenadier sergeants thrived on, I don't think!

When the battalion was formed up and ready for inspection, we heard the chinking of spurs drawing nearer to the parade ground and gradually the faint sound of cultured feminine voices too. Then the sergeant major called the battalion to attention, and we gave a royal salute. (I was quite proud of my second F flute harmony part that day. It sounded like the music of the gods in my ear!)

A story then unfolded which was to echo throughout the regiment for years to come. Our colonel approached the Corps of Drums with a huge entourage of the field marshall, our commanding officer (Lieutenant Colonel Johnny Nelson), the senior major, Captain and

Adjutant M. S. Bayley, Sergeant Major Les Burrell, and our Drum Major 'Swivel' Petersen. (He was so called because of his nervous habit, when on parade, of swivelling on his heels slightly to pluck at his trousers for some reason known only to him! We used to refer to this nervous habit as his 'three-quarter roll and crutch adjuster'!) All went swimmingly until Her Royal Highness stopped in front of our tenor drummer—a certain Ben 'Jughead' Tomlinson. After looking him up and down, she asked him how long he had been in the regiment.

'Just over three years, Your Royal Highness.' Then she remarked on the size of his instrument and asked him its name.

'It's a tenor drum, mam.' (OK up to now then.) But the lovely lady then said, 'It looks very heavy. How much does it weigh?' Back came the famous reply from Jughead, which would haunt him forever: 'Dunt knaw, sir!' in a broad Yorkshire accent. (He hailed from Hull.) Poor old Tomlinson's name rattled down the line in whispers, until eventually, the sergeant in waiting answered the command reaching him. 'Sir! Drummer Tomlinson, inattentive on parade, sir!' Poor old Jughead! I kept in touch with him for years at his home in Hull when I settled down in Yorkshire on retiring from the fire service, and we corresponded regularly until his passing in the late nineties.

The sergeants' mess photograph with Her Royal Highness is still treasured by me, not only for its historic connection, but also because whenever I look at it I can't help chuckling at the three drum sergeants in service dress standing in the centre rank. They all look to be the same height, but only I know that little John Tilbury was standing on a big breeze block to level us up! Tom and I linked hands behind John in case he showed signs of toppling off his perch!

After the photograph, we all trooped into the mess for drinky-poos with our colonel and her ravishingly beautiful younger sister, who at twenty-one was the same age as myself. She was soon surrounded by a gaggle of the younger members obviously mesmerised by her beautiful blue eyes and a very real sense of humour accompanied by a delightful cheeky grin.

There was a proud moment for our pioneer Platoon Lance Sergeant Duggie Ashfield, who was very talented artist. He had produced a most beautiful black-and-white sketch of Her Royal Highness, mounted and wearing the blue ceremonial uniform which she had worn when we last did the King's Birthday Parade on Horse Guards in 1947. After admiring the sketch for a few moments and speaking to Duggie, she asked her lady in waiting for a pen and autographed the bottom of the drawing ELIZABETH. That work of art was duly framed and hung in a place of honour on the mess anteroom wall, and it was still there when I left the regiment and the battalion in 1960. I wonder if it still hangs there now?

Leaping forward in time to April 1986, I had the temerity to write to Her Majesty the Queen to offer my loyal greetings on the occasion of her sixtieth birthday and took the opportunity to mention her visit to the battalion in Tripoli. When the answer arrived (as they always do), I knew that the Queen had seen my letter, for her private secretary said that 'Her Majesty recalls the occasion very well and remembers that there seemed to be more sand in the air than there was underfoot!'

Do I remember the start of the fifties? How can I ever forget!

CHAPTER 20
TRIPOLI IN ANOTHER AGE!

SOME YEARS AGO, AS I wrote the first draft for this book, the news on TV told of Ghadaffi's last stand to defend the armed compound of Bab al-Azziza. I thought back to September 1951, at the point of Ghadaffi's last stand it was just about sixty years prior, when the First Battalion Grenadier Guards was spending the last six weeks of the three years and three months Tripoli tour kicking our heels in Azzizia Barracks, waiting for the troopship *Devonshire* to dock and take us home to Blighty again. I spent most of that weary wait being driven mad with prickly heat!

We had moved down into the Tripoli suburb from our distant Prinn Barracks when the Third Battalion arrived to relieve us. Many of them then suffered the effects of heatstroke or heat exhaustion, which caused the extra weeks to be added on our tour until they became acclimatised—mid August, and the heat was a killer!

Those barracks figured in the news during the nineties after the night strike by units of the US Air Force. Ghadaffi's headquarters building was shown on the newsreels, and I recognised the bomb-damaged building as the orderly room block of Azzizia Barracks! If the heavily armoured Bab al-Azzizia compound is as huge as reported, then it is probable that the area embraces the little estate of the married quarters just outside the barracks gate and the nearby Gialo Barracks too. This was our first station on arriving from our recent deployment with the British forces in Palestine, with the First Battalion Irish Guards occupying Azzizia.

My friends who were the First Battalion in those years would no doubt have been trying to identify and relate the Arabic street names against the Italian names they had when we there—Green Square is easy: Il Piazza Italia. (Our NAAFI club was in the castello there). And I guess that as the triumphant rebel forces were reported as entering the city down the main street from the west into the square, I suggest they are referring to Il Corso Vittorio Emmanuelle. All who had served with the First Guards Brigade in Tripoli until King Idris was overthrown would have been watching the photos and films from there during the news bulletins and trying to spot those old familiar places such as the Pending Python bar or Les Trois Chefs café in Corso Siciliana (best mixed grill in the city!). I was trying with interest, but the desert city we knew was unrecognisable.

When we finally arrived at Warley Barracks after a week at sea aboard the *Devonshire*, followed by a long journey by the back lines from Liverpool, we just had time to stow our kit away before pay parade. I had never been as wealthy in my life, as my total pay for our six weeks de-embarkation leave was a whopping £55 which was a flipping fortune in those days!

Palestine was followed by over three years in Libya. That was a deployment never to be forgotten — certainly not by this ninety-year-old 'desert mouse', ha ha ha!

CHAPTER 21

THE NIGHT THEY WERE SLEEPING IN THE MALL

FEBRUARY 1952 FOUND ME standing with the guard of honour from the King's Company of the Grenadier Guards in Friary Court, at Saint James's Palace. I watched in awe as the colourful procession of heralds in their varying tabards made its way slowly along the flat roof just across from where we were positioned. I was wide awake now. It had been early reveille and everyone was a bit bog-eyed, although I had snatched a few moments of sleep on the Windsorian coach that had conveyed the Corps of Drums from our station at Victoria Barracks down to Wellington Barracks on Birdcage Walk, Westminster. From there we had marched with the regimental band and the King's Company up the Mall to Saint James's Palace. The period of court mourning had begun, so the colour was cased and all the drums encased in black crepe to hide the emblazoning, with all the drum braces slackened to make the drum beats muffled. The officers were wearing a wide band of black crepe on the left sleeves of their blue-grey greatcoats. I was glad of my own greatcoat and the white woollen mittens too. I don't think many of us had properly acclimatised ourselves to our cold native land yet, for it was only five months since we had arrived back in Blighty after almost four years in the searing heat of Libya and the Western Desert area of North Africa, with some time on active service in Palestine before that!

The *click-click* of the heralds' shoes was sure to attract the attention of Drill Sergeant Chinny Felton, standing to our rear, and ensure that he didn't detect any slight untoward shifting of our gaze from the regulation 'straight to the front'. Any eye movement was carefully hidden by the fringes of our bearskin caps. Anyway, history was about to be made after all!!

The Garter King at Arms unrolled a scroll of parchment and began to read out the proclamation to us, the nation, and the world. In sombre yet clearly audible words he informed that, consequent upon the death of our late well-beloved King George VI, we now, by the grace of God, had a new sovereign ascending to the throne, Her Royal Highness the Princess Elizabeth, who was now and henceforth to be styled as Her Majesty Queen Elizabeth II. Right there and then, as the cheers died away, drowned out by the regimental band playing the national anthem ('God Save the Queen' now, of course) and as the guard of honour presented arms for the royal salute, fifteen months of the most exciting time of my service with the First Battalion Grenadier Guards began. We were to be involved right at the heart of the preparations for the coronation to be held at Westminster Abbey on 2 June the following year of 1953.

There were to be months and months of preparation for the armed forces generally over the intervening period and in particular for all us of the Household Brigade (Foot Guards and Household Cavalry) beginning with the funeral of the late king at Saint George's Chapel in Windsor castle in a few days' time, of course. I had been involved in a practice at Windsor already for that sad occasion, together with a buddy of mine, George Duffin, a fellow lance sergeant in the Corps of Drums. We would be with the guard of honour at the foot of the steps of Saint George's Chapel and were to be responsible for dressing the King's Company colour (the Royal Standard of the Regiment) when it was uncased, bedecked with a huge black crepe bow hanging from the crown at the pike head. We were also to assist the ensign in any way that was required. The huge standard would be dipped to the ground as the coffin was borne past—that precious burden carefully carried up the steps by the eight carefully selected NCOs and guardsmen of the King's Company together with their Company Sergeant Major 'Freddie' Clutton, MM, and Second Lieutenant Naylor-Leyland. A small replica of the King's Company colour would be interred with the king in the chapel, and any new colours, badges, buttons, etc. of our regiment would then be altered to carry the cypher (ER) of the new sovereign (reversed and interlaced as per regimental custom). I heard from my dad that the moment when the bearer party was halfway up the chapel steps was captured for all time on a full double-page photograph in the *Daily Graphic*, a tabloid newspaper of the time. (It has disappeared from my possession over the years.) George and I can be seen quite clearly in our position at the rear of the guard of honour, heads bowed as the guards were 'resting on their arms reversed'. This was a rather complicated movement of arms drill, done in slow time, which finishes with the rifle butt traps uppermost and their muzzles resting on the toe caps of each member of the guard of honour. The manoeuvre was performed that day faultlessly as the guard of honour carried out a last, final solemn duty for their departed sovereign!

Later on, in the early summer, we moved from Windsor down to London where we were to be stationed in Wellington Barracks, a mere few hundred yards away from Buckingham Palace. Thousands of tourists would witness the unusual sight (at that time) of the scarlet tunics of guardsmen giving way to a richly varied assortment of uniforms worn by the hundreds of troops from the British Commonwealth, who were all to be given their chance to mount guard for twenty-four hours at a time when they started arriving in the capital in the spring of 1953.

We soon got into the swing of London duties again, although the last time we had been in the Smoke back in 1947 at Chelsea Barracks, we were wearing khaki greatcoats and service dress caps, not blue-grey greatcoats and bearskins! In 1947, the battalion had not long been back from Germany and WWII. Now things were much altered following the release back to civilian life of thousands of guardsmen. The Guards Armoured Division was but a proud memory, and the Household Brigade was reduced to just eleven battalions, viz. three Grenadier Guards, three Coldstream Guards, two Scots Guards, two Irish Guards, and one Welsh Guards.

Life was starting to be more cheerful in the England of the early fifties (barring the sadness surrounding the death of our late king, of course). Although there was still a rationing of certain food commodities as during the recent wartime, living was getting a little easier. All during that summer, autumn and winter of 1952 we established ourselves as the host battalion accommodating the planners (artisans and ceremonial staff alike) for the forthcoming Coronation to take place the next year. To prepare us for the long distances that were planned for the coronation procession routes, we were taken slowly up though a programme of marching various distances—in all manner of orders of dress, dependent on the prevailing weather. When we took part in the actual coronation procession itself, the marching was second nature to us and the soles of my feet were almost as tough as the boots that protected them!

Two exciting events took place during that same year of 1952, and I never tire of recalling them and talking about them to anyone caring to listen.

In August, twenty-five members of the Corps of Drums assembled at the recording studio of Decca Records, where we were to act as a backing group for both sides of a Vera Lynn release. At the door of the studio reception, we were met by the studio manager and a young lady, presumably his secretary or clerk of sorts, as she carried a black leather attaché case. After our welcome to Decca and a brief explanation of the afternoon's programme, we made our way into the studio proper, filing past the lady clerk who gave us our pay for the gig—we each received a £1 note, and that included the drum major (he had a voice like a dog anyway!). We found ourselves in a surprisingly small room, with walls clad with a sort of board covered in holes. Johnny Johnstone, the leader of the session musical group, explained to us that it was to deaden the acoustical echoes and assist the sound engineer to produce an acceptably mixed sound for the recording. To that end he had us up doing a few sound tests, including singing a verse of a song we knew. We all opted for our own 'The British Grenadiers', of course! Then the star herself came out to meet us and put us at our ease, as only the Forces' Sweetheart knew how, by speaking and laughing with us all. She was charming and sweet, just as we expected. Knowing that she had been singing to the forces all through the war years, we were expecting a middle-aged lady, but she was only in her mid thirties (we supposed). Vera was only wearing a minimum of make-up, not plastered with grease paint as we had expected; and for the 'getting to know you' session, she had some curlers in her hair!

That afternoon, we sang our hearts out for Vera just as the Coldstreamers had done before us when she recorded 'Auf Wiedersehn' with them in the background. The two songs that Vera recorded with us that afternoon were 'You Belong to Me' and 'The Old Windsor Waltz'. I don't know whether it was our singing or not, but the record never reached the charts as such, but we did get 'You Belong to Me' on the radio now and again. What a flop! Probably if Decca had given us two quid each instead of only one . . . Who knows? We might still be getting an airing now and again on the wireless!

Long before the modern *Royal Variety* show, it was the custom for the sovereign to attend a variety show at the Palladium theatre on more formal lines, although comprising top-line acts and artistes. It was called *The Royal Command Variety Performance*, and it was always held in November. In the month of the show, I was one of a party of six guardsmen from the battalion chosen to take part in the very first *Royal Command Variety Performance* of the young queen's reign. All day long, we sat in the stalls of the theatre watching and listening to famous artistes that some of us had only heard of until then. We heard Jonny Rae singing 'Crying in the Rain' and 'Little White Cloud That Cried'. I was able to satisfy my mum's curiosity when she asked me. 'Yes, Mum, he did cry when singing, and yes, he does wear hearing aids!' Our companions in the stalls for most the time when they weren't on stage were the Beverly Sisters, who were lovely, friendly and very giggly, especially when one of our gang of guardsmen told them a rather risqué joke!

We were also entertained by the lovely Gracie Fields and the Crazy Gang (they were a hoot! I'm sure they were playing straight to us!). A special treat came when we were in with the wardrobe mistress and getting kited out with our old-time soldiers' costumes (I was a Tudor soldier in breastplate and bloomers, carrying a pike!) We were visited by one of the artistes at his request, and for almost a quarter of an hour the great Josef Locke himself forgot his stage persona and reverted to his old identity of Lance Sergeant J. McLochlan of the Irish Guards. ('Once a guardsman, always a guardsman' in his case!)

There was a roving newshound back stage, and sensing a story, he got myself and a guardsman, who (like me) came from Yorkshire, to pose with about six of the Tiller Girls (all Yorkshire lasses themselves) who were dressed as French poodles with little French pom-poms where it mattered! He got them to be draped all over us (perfumed heaven!) and started clicking away with his camera. My mum bored the neighbours to death in the pub with that photo from the *Yorkshire Evening Post*!

We were part of the opening chorus, straight after the Tiller Girls display of their high kicks. (Those girls could really dance!) Then, for the first time on stage since the death of the late Queen Victoria, we sang out at the tops of our loyal guardsman voices 'The Soldiers of the Queen', and we heard that the royal family loved it! It wouldn't be true to say that I have dined out on my story of the foregoing experience, but it has certainly earned me a pint or two in many differing places over the years!

We had a thriving social life in the sergeants' mess during 1952 including, in June, when the major part of our dining facilities moved lock, stock, and barrel for a week into a marquee on the grassy area facing the main grandstand at Ascot Racecourse for Royal Ascot week. Quite close to the rails too, so we had a good view of the racing. What a privilege it is to be a member of the Household Brigade! I lashed out 5s. (25p) each way on a horse I fancied because of its name, Fur Baby. It struck me that as we wore bearskin caps, something was telling me it was a cert. It is still running somewhere I think! That was my very first flutter on the gee-gees, and my last (until I was settled in civilian life some years later). We had a shuttle service of battalion three-tonners going backwards and forwards to Ascot all week, so it was easy enough to arrange transport after guard mounting, a lovely week.

Our regimental band had the sole privilege of providing the music for the royal flower show at Chelsea every summer too in those days, and it was easy to arrange to go with a friend in the band to sneak me on to their coach from Wellington Barracks one afternoon so that I could 'listen to the band, me old mate'.

I enjoyed a leisurely stroll around the various exhibits, learning quite a lot about the wonders of horticulture. The music from the band area sounded great, and I enjoyed a nice cream tea with the band for free because I was dressed in my blue patrols, I think!

After returning from our Christmas privilege leave (how many times had I to explain to the youngsters in the Corps of Drums, 'You get your leave as a privilege laddie. It is *not* a right'), and with the start of the the new year, things began moving more quickly towards the coronation in June. There were troops arriving from all over the Commonwealth every week although we had just a few in Wellington Barracks from two Canadian regiments, the PPCLI (Princess Patricia's Canadian Light Infantry) and a regiment from the French-speaking part of Canada, the Royal Twenty-Second Regiment of Canada, who were always referred to as the Vandoos — a derivation from the French for twenty-two.

I was never off the piano in the mess, it seemed, and neither did I have to buy a drink either, life was great! The Vandoo sergeants used to get the mess bouncing with rousing choruses of 'Alouette', and it was many years before the words for 'Maple Leaf' faded out of my memory! We also had a couple of Kiwis from the New Zealand Army (complete with their Baden-Powell pointed caps) in the sergeants' mess. One was a Maori, and he tried to teach me how to roll my eyes and grimace one evening in the Maori tribal greeting fashion. I gave it up after a few minutes, going back to the piano with stinging eyes! I think that the Australians were in another barracks somewhere —Hounslow, maybe?

Many of the troops and horses from overseas were encamped all over London District, and a huge number of them were billeted in the vast London air raid shelter called Clapham Deep. It could accommodate hundreds and had tired beds, ablutions, latrines, and cooking facilities. Someone had put a block on its dismantling until after the coronation, and it solved a huge accommodation problem for the QMG staff at London District, I bet.

As mentioned previously, it had been decided that the visiting Commonwealth troops would be offered the singular honour (at that time) of finding the Queen's Guard at Buckingham Palace and Saint James's too, and unless they had a band of their own, we would play them across from Wellington Barracks with a Guards band and Corps of Drums. This was to continue throughout the time leading up to a couple of weeks before the coronation was to take place on the 2nd June. When taking the new guard on for the Changing of the Guard ceremony at Buckingham Palace, part of the approach for the new guard is to enter the palace forecourt by the gate at the Constitution Hill end, where the band does a left wheel, and the new guard a left form into line, then halt. After dressing had been carried out to the satisfaction of the accompanying drill sergeant, the whole body of band and guards advanced in slow time for fifteen paces, playing the first eight bars of the regimental slow march. The Grenadier Guards, of course, go forward to the march 'Scipio' so it was rather a change to go forward to 'Waltzing Matilda' or the 'Maple Leaf'. I had to wonder also how many months those visitors had been practising for just this particular occasion. They were faultless with their drill and deportment and their immaculate appearance too — they were great ambassadors for their countries, who had every cause to be proud of their troops at the palace that year!

I remember that the Pakistani troops had their own very large pipe band in scarlet jackets and blue trousers which were tucked into calf-length white gaiters. On their heads they wore striped pattern turbans with huge starched red frills sticking up at the right hand side. The band was fronted by their drum major, who had the biggest moustache I had ever seen, waxed and sticking out straight to a point on each side of his face. I swear it was every bit of twenty-four inches from tip to tip!

The Pakistani new guard following behind their band was a careful-sized body of smart men in khaki battle dress (no web anklets on this occasion), all wearing turbans similar to the band. The obvious difference was that their turbans were khaki, including the starched frills. Fate was to prove unkind for the Pakistani troops that day, for they had no sooner got to the point in the changing over where the corporals go off to post the oncoming sentries than a light but persistent rainfall began to fall and prevailed for the remainder of the proceedings. The Pakistani soldiers remained impassively staring straight ahead, with nary a movement in their ranks. But it soon became clear to the tittering hundreds at the palace railings that the rain was having an unfortunate effect on the turban frills which slowly yet predictably began to sag and droop until they were hanging down the side of each soldier's face. The odd titters of the spectators soon changed to applause, however, in tribute to the rocklike steadiness of the unfortunate new guard! Come the next day, however, when they were dismounting as the old guard, every frill was starched and standing proudly on those turbans, and the sun was shining on every man!

There was a regimental cook in both of the guardroom kitchens at Buckingham palace and Saint James's. I remember the fuss that the cook at Saint James's made when the Gurkha detachment insisted on using their own cook for their own twenty-three-hour period of duty and then left one of his cooking utensils stained by the yellow saffron which they used in their food!

Meantime, away from the military activities in and around London, there was a great deal of activity in the architects and building departments of the capital generally but that of Westminster in particular.

There were miles of tiered spectator seating on both sides of the coronation procession route to and from Westminster Abbey and a particularly well-thought-out erection of wooden tiered seating inside the abbey itself, towering from the floor of the nave right up into the upper reaches of the vast west window, with slightly lower versions along the north and south reaches of the abbey walls. When it came to the matter of testing the abbey seating to ensure the safe accommodation of many exalted and velvet-covered posteriors, the battalion marched from Wellington Barracks along Birdcage Walk to the huge edifice of Christianity in the city of Westminster. Once inside the abbey, the Grenadiers, together with some Scots Guardsmen and Coldstreamers too, were spaced at regular intervals along the wooden seated accommodation. We in the Corps of Drums took up a playing formation in the central space of the transept near the chancel steps, and as soon as the sergeant major gave the orders 'Battalion . . . 'Shun!' followed by 'Quick mark time!' we struck up with a great five-pace roll and started playing one of our best quick marches. But play as loud as we might, it was only the time-beater who could make himself heard above the crashing of hundreds of army boots hammering up and down on the wooden surfaces. When the commanding officer, the brigade major, garrison sergeant major, and our own sergeant major were satisfied that the seating was well and truly tested, the music was cut off, and off we went back to barracks, where we were dismissed. The men went off to the mess room for their dinners, members of the sergeants' mess to their midday meal, and the officers to lunch. Even our meals have a social classification in the Brigade of Guards.

The pièce de résistance of all the coronation preparations for me was the most marvellously beautiful tracery of delicate white trellising archways, each surmounted by a gilded crown, running the entire length of the Mall from the Victoria Memorial all the way up to the Admiralty Arch itself.

To add to the display of architectural pageantry in the Mall, both sides of the roads along every single mile of the processional route was lined by white standards, each with it's own arm stretching out over the roadside and bearing one of the many assorted national flags of every single country in the British Commonwealth of Nations!

This was intended to be that great national occasion which would give the British people —and the millions of those living overseas who claimed our sovereign as theirs too — the chance they needed to cast off at last the shackles, restrictions, and everyday gloom which had until then been hanging over us all since the end of WWII. It was a united day of rejoicing.

On the day before the coronation, the commanding officer ordered that the entire battalion (married pads also) would be on the gate, i.e. restricted to the confines of barracks from 23.59 hours, after which every man would be within the barracks walls until the great day dawned.

Well . . . Not so, for a certain pair of gold sergeants of the Corps of Drums who, despite the very nature of their calling within the battalion, lost all sense of time as they wandered among the thousands of people in all sorts of national dress who thronged the Mall on both sides, determined to sleep there in order to be able to claim some sort of vantage point along the procession route the next day. There was a great atmosphere everywhere as my buddy Tom Cornall and I strolled among the hurricane lamps, primus stoves, pipe smoke, smells of frying bacon, singing, and above all else, the constant sound of joyous laughter from people who were out for a good time. As we got towards the top of the Saint James's Park pavement, we stopped — two Grenadier Guards sergeants wearing smartly pressed khaki battledress, white buff belts, scarlet infantry sashes, and above all, the covering of our red forage caps with their three brass rims of a gold sergeant on the peaks.

'All right, mate,' said Tom, 'after three. One — two — three.' And out from our throats came the time-honoured cry of every picquet officer in the battalion mess rooms: 'Any complaints?' Any individual replies were lost in a great sound of laughter and applause! I'll never forget that night in the United Kingdom! Realising we were pushed for time; we made our way around the back of barracks to where the anteroom windows of the sergeants' mess overlooked the road at ground-floor level until we spied one open in the bar area. Tom gave me a leg up and I managed to get up on to the window ledge with my legs astride the sill. Glancing around the fairly empty bar (it might be turned 01.00, but the bar was still open and serving), I suddenly found my eyes drawn to the gimlet eyes and hawk nose of our Sergeant Major Designate Alf Dickinson. He was to take over the battalion when our present Sergeant Major, Les Burrell, was commissioned to lieutenant quartermaster after the coronation week.

'Come on, then. Grab hold, what's up?' came a hissed call from Tom on the pavement below.

'It's the Dick. He's here—in the bar!'

'Oh, bluddy hell' said Tom (or words to that effect).

Suddenly 'Well then, you'd better haul your accomplice in, hadn't you, sergeant?' came from the direction of the bar, where the Dick (as everyone called him behind his back) stood with one hand on the bar and the other held up in front of his face as he glanced at his watch. When Tom and I eventually were standing sheepishly in front of our joint nemesis, he suddenly said with a slight glint in his eye, 'Well, you're both properly dressed, I'll give you that. But in future, you will enter the mess through the door—not a window, got it?'

'Sir!' we both responded in unison.

'Good, then let's forget it. What are you drinking?' Well, it certainly was a night to remember right enough, and do you know what? although there were rumours running rife for days afterwards, no one ever discovered the identity of the two sergeants 'sent by the Guards' on that night to check on the well-being and comfort of the thousands of people, who had come down to London to watch the coronation, when they were sleeping on the Mall!

CHAPTER 22

ON LEAVING THE ARMY, WHEN THE BELLS WENT DOWN!

AFTER LEAVING THE REGIMENT in September 1960, having achieved the rank of drum major, I was employed, for a short time, as a company rep for a firm of wholesale wine and spirits merchants before I had the pleasant experience of being headhunted! The secretary of the Yorkshire branch of the Grenadiers Association was very friendly with the chief fire officer of the West Riding County Fire Service, and I was approached to consider an appointment in the brigade, firstly as an operational fireman, and secondly as a drum major to knock into shape the embryo band, pipes, and drums of the brigade. In contrast to my previous life in the regiment, this drum major's post was to be extra and outside my prime responsibilities as an operational fireman.

I passed all my entrance exams and medical before entering the training school as a raw recruit for what proved to be three months of sheer hell. The training alternated between drill ground, drill tower, firehouse, classrooms, and the swimming pool! We all had to pass our Royal Life Saving Society bronze medallion. I also passed the mandatory annual first aid exams and proudly pinned the Saint John's medallion to the left sleeve of my reefer jacket.

I finished the course in one piece, and was posted to a fire station, bursting with knowledge and about two stones lighter! Of course, the first advice I had from my watch sub-officer (equivalent to a police sergeant) was 'You can forget all that highfalutin training school stuff and do the job as I flipping well tell you, got it?' I stood rigidly to attention and agreed vehemently, 'Understood, sub!' (If he had two chromium bars on his shoulders, he was a god!)

My first posting to an operational fire station called for me being on the 24/24 duty system, which meant being on duty with my watch for twenty-four hours and then being off duty for the next twenty-four hours, with a 'rota' day off-duty every twenty-second day. This gave us a precious three days clear of duty and a chance for a lie in bed one morning now and again —bliss! There were two duty watches on our station, Red and Blue. Each watch consisted of the sub-officer, a leading fireman, and five firemen which created a terrific esprit de corps among the seven members, as they were called on to virtually live together for six months of each year. I had the good fortune to be a member of Blue Watch, who, all except the leading fireman, were ex-servicemen. As a member of the National Fire Service during the war, the LF had been in a reserved and very necessary occupation. Winston Churchill had referred to the NFS as Britain's Fourth Arm during those terrible times of the Blitz. Our sub-officer had served on the Arctic convoys onboard a destroyer with the Royal Marines. We had another WWII ex-serviceman on the watch who had been with the wartime Royal Air Force in Malta during that island's brave siege. Then we had two former Royal Navy ratings, one had served aboard the battleship HMS *Vanguard* and the other as a stoker on HMS *Barham*. The last, but by no means the least, two members of the watch had served in HM *Brigade of Guards*, one as a guardsman in the Coldstream Guards, and myself from the Grenadier Guards. All of us formed a disciplined, tough bunch capable of taking any hard knocks that the operations of a demanding service would call on us to absorb.

I would rather attend a twenty-pump mill fire well alight and going well than turn out on a dark rain-filled night in response to the bells going down for a pile-up involving several vehicles with persons trapped. One of the stations I served at in Yorkshire covered a long stretch of the A1—the Great North Road. It was a treacherously busy road, so much so that we came to regard it as a motorway without motorway restrictions! I never served a tour of duty there without having to attend at least one road smash, and I often had to carry out the grim task of getting casualties out of the mangled wreckage of their vehicles without causing them too much distress.

Life as an operational fireman was a demanding and quite often risky undertaking. When the chance came to pass my driving test to drive the station's two fire appliances, I grasped the new role eagerly. When it was my turn to drive it relieved me from a few bouts of hectic running and climbing ladders, etc. which was always the case when we arrived on a fire ground in response to the bells going down in the station. The bells added urgency to the fire alarm, or shout, as we referred to a call for help via a 999 telephone call.

The duties of the driver on arrival at a fire ground or road smash were to site the appliance on a good, hard standing if possible, engage the pump gear, and after helping to slip and pitch the escape ladder, connect the hose from a nearby hydrant and stand by to deliver water to the men on the branch pipes. Quite often we would have to work from open water or a fire tank. This entailed connecting the heavy lengths of suction hose to the appliance and lifting water up to the pump. Although we referred to them as suction hoses, there was no sucking of water involved. The driver engaged the primer of his pump which evacuated all the air from the suction hose until a vacuum was created. This, in turn, allowed the atmospheric pressure to exert force down on the surface of the water, into the vacuum and into the appliance pump, where engine revs gave additional pressure to the water being delivered to the men on the branch pipes. We didn't spend our time playing snooker as some misguided folks supposed! Unless they themselves had, for instance, driven a Rolls Dennis F12 Pump Escape Fire Engine at eighty miles per hour with a crew of seven on board and tons of ladders and fire-tackling equipment stowed, while dealing with the added joys of mastering a crash gearbox, then they just didn't know what they were talking about!

We were sometimes called upon to deal with fatalities in the course of our duties, and we treated them all with the professional dignity and tenderness which tragedy calls for, not one of us could fail to have inward feelings of sympathy for the victims and the families who would grieve. On return to the station, however, we would all laugh and joke as we had that welcome mug of tea. We weren't being callous, for if we had allowed every job involving fatalities to stay in our thoughts, we wouldn't be fit for the role for long. Child casualties were the most traumatic that we were called upon to remove from fires and road crashes, and not one firefighter who was a father could go home and not give his little ones that extra loving cuddle and kiss!

Quite often, the smoke and toxic fumes were so intense that the donning of a breathing apparatus was necessary. In my early days with the service, that meant the one-hour self-contained oxygen and ProtoSorb (CO_2 absorbent) BA set as worn underground by the mines rescue teams in the coal mining industry. I won't describe the chemical content of the bag on one's chest. While wearing BA, we were cut off vocally by the clips on our noses and the mouthpiece, which meant that we adopted a set of predetermined signals by means of a little bulb horn mounted on the right shoulder strap, the left one being in use by our pressure gauge, which indicated the contents left in the cylinder in atmospheres. Our eyes were protected by rubber goggles, which had a nasty tendency to mist up. In the late sixties, the Draeger Normal air BA was adopted by my brigade, which although had a slightly shorter air supply, did not entail the complicated starting-up procedure we had to observe with the proto sets. The content of the cylinder was just compressed air instead of oxygen so the after-use servicing was much simpler and less time-consuming as well. The full-face mask was a boon too, for it meant we could speak to our partner in our teams of two while we were at work in smoke-filled premises, carrying out a search-and-rescue operation or attacking a fire.

One of my shouts early on in my career was during the day. We were called to a coke-processing plant in the town of Ilkley, the place which gave rise to a well-known Yorkshire song, 'On Ilkley Moor b'aht Hat!'. The chain of moving buckets, which fed the coke-processing retorts, had developed a fault. This resulted in coal being delivered uncontrolled to the necks of the sixty-feet-high retorts, which were glowing white-hot and at risk of exploding. I must admit to having a little stage fright as my partner and I climbed the raking metal staircase up and up through the four grated platforms at each floor until we were in place to deliver a spray of high-pressure water onto the buckets in the hope of cooling the contents before they fell into the retorts. These were a bit too close for comfort from where we stood with braced legs while holding on the branch pipe with grim determination, trying to ignore the searing white heat only a few yards from our backs. Suddenly we heard the strident sounds of a whistle and a shout from the divisional officer (DO) two landings below our position: 'Out you come, lads. Leave everything. It's gonna go!'

On hearing that summons, we both dropped the branch pipe, as it was an unwanted hindrance to our escape, and promptly scrambled for safety with fire boots ringing on the metal stairs. We made a hurried exit from that flipping time bomb which was threatening major damage to property and life—especially ours! I seem to remember that although the DO started a couple of floors below us, the sudden rumbling 'whoosh' as about sixty tons of white-hot coke flashed down at our sides was enough to ensure that we beat him out of the premises, much to his surprise!

Away from my operational duties, when it came to my band role away from the fire station, it was a different story altogether — almost, but not quite a repetition of the duties I had as a grenadier drum major. Regardless of my fire service rank, what I said was adhered to implicitly. I had agreed with the leading drummer, an ex-sergeant in the Royal Marines band of the royal yacht, that the side-drummers would march in front of the band, 'like we did in the Royal Marines,' a minor point with which I had no problems. He told me later on that he had visions of me wanting the drummers to march at the back, forming the rear rank of the band 'like what you flipping guards do!' Everything else that I suggested was accepted. The band would adopt the same drill as practised in Guards regiments as opposed to the Royal Navy drill generally used in the fire brigade, and the uniforms would be as near as possible to the grenadiers' as the tailor could manage with respect.

The pipe band also marched with their own drum major, but after some discussion, the director of music agreed to my request that I should be the senior drum major, so on went the crown above my four reversed chevrons and drum at the bottom of my sleeve.

CHAPTER 23

OH! FOR A CLOSER
WALK WITH GOD

THE YEARS ROLLED BY, and after a climb up the promotional ladder, and much travelling around the country, I became a Divisional Officer and Course Director at The Fire Service College in Moreton-in-Marsh, Gloucestershire, moving there with my dedicated wife and our two daughters.

I was determined to enjoy being involved with the lovely Ethos of Moreton that I had discovered previously during an appointment there from 1975 to 1978. I loved the many friends I made as a regular at the local pub the Duke of Wellington (the 'Welly') and enjoyed the company of it's Landlords and the patrons. Firstly, Molly and Ralph were in situ as Landlords in charge of the bar, followed by Tom and Beryl Pratley. It was great to be involved as a 'regular' and we once raised enough money to buy a specially adapted Tricycle for a young local laddie to help him with his mobility. I also remember well the huge guffaws from 'the gang' as I staggered past the Welly dressed as a Pumpkin. I was collecting for charity (with a heavily laden bucket!) as part of the carnival procession in town. It was raining quite hard and my costume, being made of sponge rubber, absorbed lots of weighty rainwater so I was almost on my knees by the time the procession reached the Football Club!

I have fond memories of the Aunt Sally being played on the lawn at the rear of the Welly and customs like the 'Thrift Club' which was such a boon when Christmas came round. I dressed as Santa one year too, handing out small gifts from the 'Welly' mums and dads to their little ones, as they sat conveniently near with liquid refreshment.

As we settled back into life in Moreton, and grew to love all that it involved, the family became members of the congregation of St David's Parish Church. This is a beautiful 14th century edifice built in the mellow Cotswold stone which is the hallmark of many of the farms, houses and cottages etc all over this beautiful County. I joined the small choir in the church and became the choirmaster too. We would have a weekly practice on Friday afternoons in the church after the children came out of our adjacent St David's C of E Primary and Infants' school where both of my girls were pupils. We became quite passable for a small country village choir with six adults and 11 children. One of the little ones approached me one Sunday morning to say that he 'loved the smell of his cassock'. The few choir robes that the church possessed had been augmented with loans from another parish and the smell he liked was mildew. I didn't spoil things by revealing this to the little chap with a penchant for the smell of decay!

One day I was approached by the Rector, the lovely Tom Ekin, who asked if I was still reaching out for ordination. I had never given up my wish in that direction. While I was happily involved in singing in my lifetime and even in my youth, there had always been a growing feeling that there was something missing. This had first become clear back at the tender age of 17 when I was serving as a Drummer Boy in the Guards. My Padre, Denys Browning came into my life for the first time, to become my friend and mentor right up to his death at the age of 90 in 1999. All the boy soldiers had to attend Church parade every Sunday. I started acting as a server at the midweek Communion services too. After attending scripture sessions with Denys, he eventually felt he had identified my 'calling' and took me before the Army ordination council in Dean's yard, Westminster Abbey. It was an unsuccessful experience of course for one so young, although they did invite me to try again when I was 21 years of age. Denys suggested to me that I instead leave the Army, on a Class 'B' release, to study at the Community of the Resurrection in Mirfield (back in my home county of Yorkshire) with a view of eventual ordination and probably becoming an Army Padre like himself. My army career took me along other pathways, and I did not leave on that Class B release. But here I was many years later, and Tom's nudge had awoken the call again. I studied for 12 months with him, shadowing his work and worship, often utilising my flexi time at the college to read the offices with him and spending many hours in discussion with him in his study. I had mentioned my awakened calling in a letter to my old Padre and Mentor Denys Browning, who was by this time a Priest in Papua, New Guinea. He felt compelled to reveal my divorced status. Though at that time I had been married to Babara for many years, I got a shock when Tom said one day, 'I wasn't aware the that you were a divorcee Rod' (he always called me that).

'Why yes' I replied, 'does it matter?'......

'Yes, old friend', he said to me with a sad but gentle warmth, 'I'm afraid it does in the eyes of the church, Canon law forbids the ordination of divorcees!'. Placing a comforting hand on my shoulder he assured me he would do all he could to help. Tom tried to make a special case in my name to the Director of Ordinands in the Gloucester Diocese, stressing the fact that it was my wish to be a non - stipendiary priest eventually, while still following my career as a Fire Service Officer. Coupled with the expected refusal to admit me as an ordinand was a gentle encouraging remark to the effect that 'God still has work for you in his chancel' so I assumed from this that Tom had mentioned my position as Choirmaster and my success in getting the church affiliated to the Royal School of Church Music.

When the time came for me to leave the Fire Service and our reluctant return to Yorkshire, I joined the choir at St Mary's Parish church in our village of Gomersal, together with all the family. Quite soon I developed an excellent relationship with the Organist and Choirmaster Stuart Schofield, who gave me the 'nod' to work with the juniors in the choir. Because I was unoccupied on Monday afternoons, I resumed my previous system of choir practice as the school finished at 4pm, and it proved to be a great success. I took the children, and taught them about the scriptures, the church organisation, architecture, and the RSCM (Royal School of Church Music). We had 21 juniors in the choir eventually and when I moved to my most recent church, of St Paul in Drighlington, St Mary's had a lovely choir and a dedicated membership of adults and juniors.

I joined the choir at St Pauls, of course, in December 1989 and my singing was very enjoyable as a member of a fairly large and well qualified group of singers (4 part harmony) under the guidance of a dedicated and very long serving Organist and Choirmaster George Gomersal MBE who is sadly no longer with us.

My ability to carry on singing in the choir stalls became more difficult as my mobility problems proved to be an issue. If I ever visit Church these days, it is always within the congregation as a sitting tenor! Apace with my singing, I was actively engaged in the 'divorced clergy measure' campaign. When we won our case, I was over the age of 65 and felt that for me the time had past and I was too old to continue with my wish to serve in the ministry. I must confess however to having a few pangs of regret when I have been close to others who have been through their training as Ordinands and when I was at St Mary's in the 80s, I used to have a few ordinands from the community at Mirfield visit me at home in their free study time on Wednesday afternoons. The beautiful service of Ordination of Deacons and Priests which I have attended in the cathedral takes me back in my mind to what might have been. I do not know what kind of a Priest I would have been, only God knows that, and he is keeping that opinion to himself!

CHAPTER 24

KISMET

IT WAS A WARM afternoon in 1959, and Her Majesty the Queen and HRH the Duke of Edinburgh were returning to London after their state visit to Canada. As is the custom on these state occasions, both detachments of the Queen's Guard were preparing to provide the guard of honour in the Inner Quadrangle of Buckingham Palace.

The Queen's Company of the First Battalion Grenadier Guards were finding both the Buckingham Palace and Saint James's Palace detachments, and the regimental band and the Corps of Drums were marching at the head of the Saint James's Palace detachment with the Queen's Colour of the battalion as they marched down the Mall to Buckingham Palace. As it was a state occasion, the drum major was wearing his state dress as a drummer to the royal household.

As the drum major strutted his stuff down the Mall to the stirring lilt of the march 'Trombones to the Fore', it would have been impossible for him to spot individuals among the mass of spectators lining the route. If he had, he might have noticed a young teenage lassie from Lancashire standing there with her mother. They were visiting London for the day while her father was attending a driving examiners' meeting at Hendon Police College. Our young lady had never seen the guards up close, and she was not aware either that fate was strutting almost within touching distance from her, in his coat of gold!

Onwards in time to the mid sixties and the same young lady was now employed at the headquarters of the West Riding County Fire Service, in Birkenshaw near Bradford, as an audio/shorthand typist in the fire prevention department of the brigade.

Being a contributing kind of person, she was also the secretary of the headquarters' Sports and Social Club. It was while carrying out her activities for the club that she came into contact with the social club rep from the recruit training school, one of the sub-officer instructors. It became quite usual for them to have a drink and a game of cards or dominoes in the HQ club bar and enjoyed long conversations. It was during one of those chats that the sub-officer told her of his prior life before the fire brigade, when he had been a drum major in the Grenadier Guards. After a while, they realised that she was that young teenager in 1959 who had been standing in the Mall with her mother watching, as the now fire service sub-officer in his army days, marched past as a drum major!

Friendship warmed into love, and on 20 February 1971, they were married and embarking on a deliriously happy marriage which would be blessed by two beautiful baby daughters. Barbara and I have now been married for nearly fifty-years!

I had a long, happy and varied career within the Fire Service, seeing postings within my home country of Yorkshire, to the rolling hills of the beautiful Cotswolds where I was a Course Director at the Fire Service college, Moreton-In-Marsh. There was a time during my Fire Service years when I was posted to the chilly and often Snowy highlands of Scotland. There I lived and worked accompanied, as always, by my dedicated wife Barbara and our eldest daughter Victoria. It was during our time in Aberdeen that my youngest daughter, Rebecca, joined us and our little family of four was complete.

There are many tales to tell of my years within the Fire Service and since my retirement, but in all honesty they are another complete book, yet to be written, the contents of which are bubbling away constantly within the happy memories I hold dear and think of often in my daily musings.

Printed in Great Britain
by Amazon

45810247R00135